ℓ349/29

THE EDINBURGH FRINGE

THE EDINBURGH FRINGE

ALISTAIR MOFFAT

Johnston & Bacon

A JOHNSTON & BACON book published by
Cassell Ltd.
35 Red Lion Square, London WC1R 4SG
and Tanfield House, Tanfield Lane, Edinburgh EH3 5LL
and at Sydney, Auckland, Toronto, Johannesburg
an affiliate of
Macmillan Publishing Co.
New York

First Published 1978

ISBN 0 7179 4245 7

Designed by Anne Davison

Filmset and printed in Great Britain by
BAS Printers Limited, Over Wallop, Hampshire

For my wife, Lindsay

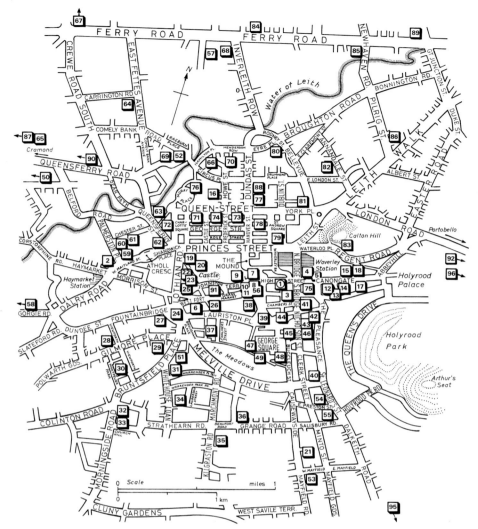

The Fringe map of Edinburgh. Each number represents a hall used for performances or exhibitions

1 Fringe Office and Fringe Club	24 Central Halls Tollcross
2 Grosvenor Centre	25 Heriot Watt Theatres
3 Adam House	26 Edinburgh College of Art
4 Old St Paul's Church Hall	27 Tollcross School
5 Netherbow Arts Centre	28 Viewforth Centre
6 Lauriston Hall	29 Darroch School
7 Saltire Society and Old	30 St Oswald Hall
Traverse at James Court	31 Old Gillespie's School
8 Celtic Lodge and Riddles	32 North Morningside Church
Court and Baden Powell House	33 Church Hill Theatre
9 Highland Church	34 James Gillespie's School
10 St Columba's by the Castle	35 Marchmont St Giles Church
11 Traverse Theatre Club	36 St Catherine's Argyle
12 St Mary's Street Hall	37 St Thomas of Aquin's School
13 Lodge Canongate Kilwinning	38 Greyfriars Kirk
14 Moray House Theatre	39 Old Chaplaincy Centre
15 Harry Younger Hall	40 Nelson Hall
16 Studio 4A, Howe Street	41 South Bridge Primary School
17 Milton House Primary School	and St Patrick's Primary
18 Calton Studios	42 Davie Street Arts Centre
19 St John's Church Hall	43 Hill Place Centre
20 St Cuthberts Church Hall	44 New Chaplaincy Centre –
21 Bartholomew & Son	site of Barrie Halls,
22 St Mark's Unitarian Church	Paperback Bookshop,
23 Little Lyceum	Pollock Hall

45 Epworth Hall	69 St Bernard's Church Hall
46 Classic Cinema	70 St Stephen's Hall
47 Catholic Chaplaincy Centre	71 Royal Arch Halls
48 11 Buccleuch Place	72 YWCA
49 George Square Theatre	73 Henderson Gallery
50 Royal High School	74 Hill Street Hall
52 Stockbridge Church	76 The Danish Institute
53 Mayfield Church Hall	77 Grant Gallery
54 St Peter's Church Hall	78 The Undercroft and St Andrew
55 Jewish Community Centre	& St George's Church
56 Central Library	79 YMCA, Royal British Hotel
57 Edinburgh Academy Prep School	and Grand Restaurant
58 Wester Hailes Community	80 Pilrig Park School
Centre	81 Cathedral Hall Albany Street
59 St Mary's Cathedral	82 Transport Hall
60 Walpole Hall	83 Calton Hall
61 11 Chester Street	84 St Serf's Church Hall
62 St George's West Church Hall	85 Coach House Theatre
63 French Institute	86 Zetland Hall
64 Broughton High School	88 Torrance Gallery
65 Dunfermline College of	89 Leith Town Hall
Physical Education	90 Hopetoun House
66 Theatre Workshop Edinburgh	92 Holyrood RC School
67 Ainslie Park School	95 Craigmillar Castle
68 St James Church Hall	96 Portobello Town Hall

 **Contents**

Part Four
1970 to 1977

 # Acknowledgements

I am indebted to the Board of Directors of the Fringe Society, who allowed me to use such of their records as remain. Most of my work has been done in the Edinburgh Room of the Central Library and I am very grateful to the staff for their interest and assistance. The staff of the Traverse Theatre Club have allowed me to search through their records, and George Bain of the Festival Society did my work for me in seeking out all references to 'Fringe' in the minutes of Festival Council meetings. I also want to thank Allen Wright and Stewart Boyd of *The Scotsman* for their help. I am grateful to my friends, Andrew Kerr and Leslie Bennie, for reading my manuscript. And finally, this book would not have appeared without the encouragement of my wife Lindsay Moffat, and the kindness and good humour of Jenny Carter of Johnston and Bacon.

Alistair Moffat, Edinburgh, January 1978

 # Introduction

The Edinburgh Fringe is the largest arts festival in the world. It grew up without any central guidance or design and my purpose in writing its history is to account for it as it developed. More than most festivals the Fringe has an air of spontaneity and transience and if this book seems to take a sober view of an annual occasion when huge numbers of people enjoy themselves, it is because I have concentrated on recording such facts as were available rather than on attempting to recreate atmosphere.

The book falls into four parts which are arranged chronologically: but within this framework events do not necessarily take place in sequence. For example, the entire history of the Traverse Theatre Club from 1963 to 1976 is inserted whole, after sections dealing with the early Sixties and before the section on the Fringes from 1963 to 1965. The brief histories of the Pool Lunch Hour Theatre Club, the 7:84 Theatre Company and Theatre Workshop Edinburgh have been incorporated in a similar way.

Finally the length of each part of the book varies in rough proportion to the amount of surviving material. The first two parts are short because the Fringe was relatively small in the early period and there is not much documentation to be found. Most of my material comes from the newspapers of the day. The last two parts are much longer not only because the Fringe grew but also because the Festival Fringe Society came into being as a central record-keeping body.

PART ONE

The Beginnings

When preparations for the first Edinburgh Festival in 1947 began, its organisers hoped to make an impact on at least two sorts of people; the general public who would make up the audiences, and the community of performers who would entertain them. What they could not have foreseen was the fact that they motivated more performers than they could accommodate in their first programme. It therefore came as a surprise that eight theatre groups turned up, uninvited and unheralded, to add their artistic efforts to the 1947 Festival. The officially sponsored performers occupied the best of Edinburgh's theatres and concert halls, leaving the first unofficial groups to avail themselves of small and sometimes unexpected theatres, located on the fringe of the Festival.

In this way two of the Fringe's defining features became clear at the outset; the use of small, intimate performing spaces, which often had to be converted into theatres by their stage crews, and groups who were not taken into the programme of the official Festival Society.

So, in this early period there was no actual Fringe programme and no central box office to sell tickets. Each group had to take its chances and try to survive on its own. At the beginning of this book it is worthwhile recording who those first ever Fringe groups were. If there had been a 1947 Fringe programme, it might have looked like the illustration overleaf.

It is unlikely that any one of these groups had the idea of performing on the Fringe and subsequently contacted the others. Glasgow Unity Theatre had definite left-wing leanings and certainly saw the first Edinburgh Festival as a largely bourgeois activity and the Fringe as an opportunity to offer theatre to the mass of people. On a more general level, it is significant that six of the first eight groups came from Scotland. Perhaps the first Fringe may be seen as a show of the strength of amateur drama in Scotland. Just after the Second World War there was an atmosphere of enterprise and missionary zeal in Scottish amateur drama, and the feeling that if a Scottish National Theatre were to come about it would need the help of the amateurs. It is not stretching the argument too far to associate the growth of the Fringe and Fringe techniques with this movement. Here is part of *The Scotsman*'s report on James Bridie's address to the Scottish Community Drama Association during the 1950 Festival:

> 'It is the two boards and a passion that counts,' he said. 'If you can do that then for heaven's sake go ahead and do it. Get some building—four walls somewhere. Get some activity going meant to help the theatre and not to help the vanity of some little team.'
>
> A county theatre could be a centre of all the arts. A barn could be made into a theatre, an apron stage could be made. It was not necessary to make little theatres facsimiles of the London Haymarket.
>
> If the Scottish theatre was to come to anything—'the Scottish theatre is not yet born'—the amateurs, lovers of the drama, must form themselves into groups in every county in Scotland.

Returning to 1947, the first Fringe would have made a respectable festival on its own and despite competition from the official programme, attendances were good and several of

The Christine Orr Players (an amateur company from Edinburgh) presented

MACBETH

at the YMCA theatre in South St Andrew Street.
The Glasgow Unity Theatre presented

The Lower Depths

by Maxim Gorky, and

The Laird o' Torwatletie

by Robert MacLellan at the Little Theatre in the Pleasance.
Edinburgh Peoples' Theatre did

THUNDER ROCK

also at the Little Theatre.
Edinburgh District Scottish Community Drama Association did

The Anatomist

by James Bridie, again at the Little Theatre.
The Pilgrim Players (from the Mercury Theatre in London) presented

The Family Reunion

and

Murder in the Cathedral

both by T. S. Eliot at the Gateway Theatre in Leith Walk.
Edinburgh College of Art Theatre Group did

by Strindberg at the YMCA.
The Lanchester Marionette Theatre performed a series of short puppet
plays in the restaurant of the New Victoria Cinema (now the Odeon)
in Clerk Street.
The Carnegie Trust sponsored a production of

EVERYMAN

which was staged in Dunfermline Cathedral.

the shows received good notices from the Press. Had these groups suffered heavy losses, the Fringe might have fizzled out there and then. Praise was heaped on the production of *Everyman* at Dunfermline Cathedral and one critic remarked that it was a shame the show was so far out 'on the fringe of the Festival'. Apart from that isolated instance, the Fringe was referred to as the 'Semi Official' element in the 1947 Festival.

The 1947 Fringe was also called 'Festival Adjuncts' so it was with some relief that both audiences and critics adopted the term 'Fringe' when it was properly coined by the playwright, Robert Kemp, in a strangely prophetic article that appeared in the *Edinburgh Evening News* on 14 August 1948. Headlined 'More that is Fresh in Drama', Kemp's preview of official drama ended with this paragraph:

Round the Fringe

The Gateway, before assembling its own permanent company in the autumn, is given over to visits from two outstanding English companies—the Glyndebourne Childrens' Theatre in 'Androcles and the Lion' by Bernard Shaw, and Martin Browne's Pilgrim Players in 'The First-Born' a new play by the young English poet and playwright Christopher Fry, on the subject of Moses.

Round the fringe of official Festival drama there seems to be more private enterprise than before. The Makars present that amusing Bridie skit on the Brains Trust and marriage 'It Depends What You Mean' in the Cygnet Theatre. In the YMCA Christine Orr's company are giving the first performances of a new play by Robin Stark, 'The Lady and the Pedlar', while later on Glasgow Unity brings a new comedy by Robert MacLellan suitably entitled 'The Flooers o' Edinburgh'. I'm afraid some of us are not going to be often at home during the evenings!

As it became clear that the Festival Society was not going to provide facilities for Fringe groups, an element of self-help began to emerge. Groups had always done their own advertising and sold their tickets at different outlets. It was not long before a sort of Fringe programme was compiled and published under the title 'Other Events' in an omnibus Festival programme produced by John Menzies. And by 1954 C. J. Cousland, an enterprising Edinburgh printer, had persuaded most Fringe groups to advertise in the first Fringe programme. This was a patchy publication with a strange cover motif and the title 'Additional Entertainments' at the top. Nevertheless Cousland's programme did assert the Fringe as an independent entity standing outside the official Festival programme.

More self-help became evident when, in 1951, a group of Edinburgh University students set up a reception centre for students attending the Festival or performing at the Fringe. Opposite the Gateway Theatre, at 25 Haddington Place, it was run by the International Student Service who provided meals and cheap accommodation. Many of the early Fringe performers used it.

The desire to promote groups more obviously and to make it easier for them to appear in Edinburgh was growing, and the demand for Fringe services, such as a central box office and a Fringe Club, intensified. *The Scotsman* during the 1953 Festival expressed its views on the relationship between Fringe and Festival:

There are, however, distinct elements of difficulty in the situation in a general sense. The sight of a four-piece accordion band playing at the kerb-side in Princes Street the other day, and, 20 yards away, three young women handing out free samples of a well-known brand of paper handkerchiefs, gave an indication of what could happen in Edinburgh at Festival time, if the position went uncontrolled.

If the Fringe were organised they could do much to help the Magistrates of the city as well as

Reproduced courtesy of Scotsman Publications

A scene from *The Flying Doctor* **performed by Theatre Workshop at the Epworth Hall as part of the Edinburgh Peoples' Festival in 1951**

maintaining the standards and atmosphere of the Festival. More immediate problems for them, however, concern the sale of tickets for their shows, advance publicity and hall accommodation.

The advantages of the latter, if not the former suggestion slowly began to make itself clear to Fringe groups.

In 1954 a meeting of Fringe groups was called. From *The Scotsman* again:

> With the purpose of organising the Fringe events, a conference of interested parties is to be held at the Moray Knox Arts Centre in the Canongate this morning. The aim is to set up an 'official' unofficial festival.
>
> The position of the promoters of Fringe events has, it would seem, reached a crucial point, and if nothing is done, it may well be that the Fringe in the future, with the exception of resident players, may consist of amateur productions.
>
> The situation at the Festival was summed up by one producer when he said: 'We are cutting each others throats.' A comment from a spokesman from another company was: 'What we require is a small organisation to act as a brain for the Fringe.' Suggestions which it is understood will be put forward at the conference this morning include the need for a central booking office for unofficial events and the placing of multiple newspaper advertisements.
>
> The London Club Theatre Group, however, do not believe that the answer is to be found in the groups getting together 'merely to be more official'. This would result, they feel, in an alternative organisation being set up which would simply increase the rift between the official and unofficial festivals. They think that any move towards helping the unofficial festival must come from official bodies, and they have declined an invitation to this morning's meeting.

Clearly the London Club Theatre Group's aspirations to become part of the official Festival were not shared by the rest of the Fringe. In 1955 Edinburgh University students took an initiative and sought permission to set up a central Fringe box office in a part of Old College, accessible off Chambers Street, opposite the new theatre at Adam House. They also provided a restaurant for Fringe performers which stayed open until 11.30 pm each night. This was located in the Examination Hall, and judging by press reports it was most welcome and very successful. The box office proved a loss-making venture, mainly because, said the students, all Fringe companies did not use it, especially professionals like Duncan MacRae's troupe and predictably, the London Theatre Club Group.

Nevertheless the idea worked well enough and was patronised by the student companies then performing on the Fringe. By 1955 Durham, Oxford, Birmingham and Edinburgh were all appearing regularly in Edinburgh at Festival time.

 # The Politics of the Early Groups

From the very first Festival onwards the Fringe has always contained a political element, either plays with a point of view to get across, or groups with a particular political persuasion. In 1947 a Marxist company, the Glasgow Unity Theatre, mounted a production of the seldom performed *The Lower Depths* by Maxim Gorky and a run of Robert MacLellan's *The Laird o' Torwatletie*. Both shows were aimed at working people as well as the regular theatre-going minority. In 1948 the same group planned to premiere *The Flouers o' Edinburgh*, also by MacLellan, in Princes Street Gardens—again to make it more accessible. By 1949, with the encouragement of Labour MP Norman Buchan and his wife Janey, Joan Littlewood's Theatre Workshop had arrived at the Edinburgh Fringe to do four plays: *The Love of Don Pemerperlin for Belisa in his Garden* by Frederico Garcia

Lorca, *The Flying Doctor* by Molière and *The Proposal* by Chekhov. All of these were done at the Epworth Hall in Nicolson Square, and all, without exception enjoyed very good houses. Their fourth production was a premiere, *The Other Animals* written by Ewan MacColl. It was about the trials of a political prisoner in a concentration camp—a fresh memory in 1949: one of the Festival performers, Gustav Grundgens, had abuse and leaflets hurled at him accusing him of being a Nazi.

Accompanying Joan Littlewood's productions were readings by famous, or notorious, Scottish poets such as Hugh MacDiarmid and Sidney Goodsir-Smith. By 1951 this co-operation had grown into the Edinburgh Peoples' Festival which was based at Oddfellows' Hall in Forrest Road and St Columba's Episcopal Church Hall in Johnston Terrace. Amongst the organisers were Norman and Janey Buchan and Jack Kane. Their aims were straightforward: they wanted to make a cultural contribution from the Labour Movement to the Edinburgh Festival, and by so doing popularise it so that the event gained a broader basis of support from a cross-section of society. The programme was comprehensive, with Theatre Workshop, the Glasgow Unity Theatre, the Barrhead Co-operative Choir, recitals promoted by St Cuthbert's Co-operative, lectures from Tom Driberg and readings from several poets, including MacDiarmid.

It is difficult to judge how well the Peoples' Festival went, because their shows seemed to be largely ignored by critics. Many make no mention of it in their Festival previews and all that seems to have been reviewed were Ewan MacColl's *Uranium 235* and *Time of Strife* done by the Unity Theatre. There were two reasons for this. First, critics felt that it was not the Fringe's role to be heavy, and second, propaganda put over in the form of plays had not yet become acceptable. R. H. Westwater wrote in the *Weekly Scotsman* during the 1953 Festival:

> ... the Fringe has given us at least some of the most valuable experiences in the series of past Festivals; the most complimentary proof possible of the real importance of the whole enterprise; and that the lighter side, so far too neglected, is an essential of all-round excellence.

This view of the Fringe as solely a frivolous and frothy exercise still persists amongst the press to a degree, but no-one now gets as upset as *The Spectator*'s critic did at the political content of Theatre Workshop's show in 1952:

> A more melancholy evening is to be spent at the Oddfellows Hall where Mr Ewan MacColl's fellow-travelling sermon called *The Travellers* is ingeniously produced by Miss Joan Littlewood. Theatre Workshop is a very motion (sic) of devotion and zeal: a good company and a good director zealously devoted to the presentation of propaganda thinly disguised as experimental drama.

The Edinburgh Peoples' Festival (always billed in the press as 'The Left Wing Edinburgh Peoples' Festival) petered out after two years but its aims to popularise the Edinburgh Festival have been realised in the Seventies with the enormous local response to the Fringe from all sections of the community. Political theatre of one sort and another has always been a feature of successive Fringe programmes, and it is perhaps one of the achievements of the Fringe that committed groups have become less unacceptable to critics and the public.

A scene from *Uranium 235* by Ewan MacColl, performed by Theatre Workshop at Oddfellows Hall as part of the Edinburgh Peoples' Festival in 1951

Reproduced courtesy of Scotsman Publications

Duncan MacRae in the premiere production of T. M. Watson's *Johnnie Jouk the Gibbet* at the Palladium Theatre in 1953

Reproduced courtesy of Scotsman Publications

 # The Scottish Element

One of the major criticisms of the early Festivals was that they did not contain an identifiably Scottish element, and that the official Festival represented a largely foreign import grafted onto an Edinburgh setting. Playwright Robert Kemp voiced this opinion in 1947, and was promptly asked to adapt Sir David Lindsay's *The Thrie Estaits* for production in the Assembly Hall. Despite this, the critics still complained about the lack of ethnic culture—they felt that more Scottish drama would build a secure local audience for the Festival.

The Fringe recognised this need early on and the mainly amateur companies (such as the Edinburgh Peoples' Theatre—no connection with the Peoples' Festival—and the Scottish Community Drama Association) began a long tradition of presenting works written both by Scots and in Scots. By 1952 professionals, in the shape of Duncan MacRae, had taken a hand, mounting T. M. Watson's *Bachelors Are Bold* at the Palladium Theatre in East Fountainbridge. The next year, he and his company premiered *Johnnie Jouk The Gibbet* also by Watson, a play much performed by amateur groups since then.

The controversy over the continuing lack of a Scottish element in the official programme was gradually coming to a head. In *The Scotsman* of 3 September 1955 Duncan MacRae levelled an accusation at Ian Hunter and the Festival Society:

> They aren't ashamed of Scotch Whisky or Arthur's Seat, but they seem to be of Scottish Drama. They almost pretend it doesn't exist . . . One of the main criticisms levelled against Scottish plays is that no-one goes to see them anyway. I have tried to make that particular criticism invalid.

MacRae's Scottishows productions at the Palladium Theatre had been very successful, having been sold out almost every night of their run. He continued his argument,

> The next step is to prove that there is a market for Scottish plays. I don't say that we have quite reached that stage. My actors should be better paid; more should be spent on scenery and lighting; everything should be done better. But we are very close to it.

MacRae in the words of *The Scotsman* reporter,

> He was all for the Festival, but thought the prime responsibility of the Festival Society was to put on something Scottish. It was most unfair to say that they had never been offered a brilliant Scottish play. In his opinion some of the plays they had put on had been rather short of first class.
>
> If the Festival were to be anything other than merely a commercial proposition, Scottish events must be the heart of it. As host the least we could do was to show what we could do ourselves, but this was a responsibility the Festival Society had not fulfilled.

Ian Hunter's reply was that the Festival had not been offered any Scottish play which was good enough to be included in the Festival programme. However, there was much Scottish drama that was good enough for the Fringe. *The Scotsman* again:

> Mr Hunter said that Duncan MacRae in the shows he was putting on at the Palladium Theatre, was making an extremely big contribution to the Edinburgh Festival, and whether it was official or unofficial was, in a sense, immaterial.

This last comment shows two things; first that the Festival Society had by 1955 recognised the Fringe as an integral (but not integrated) part of the Edinburgh Festival, and second that it was the proper home for Scottish drama. The sheer volume of Scottish plays done on the Fringe since 1947 is certain evidence of one of the Fringe's most lively and important facets—as a platform for Scottish drama.

The Unicorn Players appeared at the first Fringe in 1947 and had an unbroken run of annual successes until 1956. Plays written about Edinburgh, past and present, were their forte. This is a scene from *Mrs Scott of Castle Street*; **the shy young man second from the left is Leonard Maguire**

 # Relations with the Official Festival

During this early period critics tended to characterise the Fringe as a poor, but sometimes inspiring relation of the official Festival. It was seen very much as a sideshow and when a Fringe show received a good notice (and many did) it was regarded as an unexpected and welcome extra to the standard fare on offer at the larger auditoria. In 1948 and again in 1949 the Festival programme carried information on 'Other Events' which included some of the unofficial shows.

The actual relationship between the Festival and the Fringe was, in the early years, more avuncular than competitive. Most groups (there were several honourable exceptions) regarded official shows as naturally superior and a standard to be aimed for rather than shot at. The Festival Society was much gratified by its unofficial counterpart and the paranoia of later years was not yet in evidence. In 1951 Ian Hunter, the second Festival Director, expressed his views to *The Edinburgh Evening News*:

> Regarding the dramatic companies 'on the fringe of the Festival' Mr Hunter said that from the artistic point of view, he personally and unreservedly welcomed the upsurge of enthusiasm and talent which the Festival proper had brought about. To what extent the Society would wish to bring these 'fringe' companies into the comity of the Festival proper was still to be discussed but he thought the Society did appreciate the excellence of quality of some of the performances which had been given.

Edinburgh Festival Fringe Society 1959

The distinguished English Actress and Broadway Star

Rosalinde Fuller

in Subject to Love

HER OWN DRAMATIZATION OF WORKS BY Dickens. Mansfield. Maupassant. Chekhov. Dostoievsky. Kipling. Zola. Schnitzler.

"Rosalinde Fuller's performance is wonderfully unhackneyed, unfamiliar, and unmonotonous . . . She has successfully toured Europe and North America with these dramatized Stories, and recently captivated Israel and fascinated the Persian Gulf. Miss Fuller can easily spread her conquests further still."

Alan Dent. "News Chronicle"

Y. M. C. A.   THEA[TRE]

South St. Andrew Street, EDINBURGH. 2.

Mondays to Fridays at 2.45 p.m.

August 24th to September 4th, inclusiv[e]

TICKETS 5/-   MAY BE OBTAINED AT THE BOX OFFICE

Prior to Scandinavian Tour

Balliol Dramatic Club, Oxfo[rd]

THE ALCHE[M]IST

by

BEN J[ONS]ON

Kirk[...all (... C]owgate)

[...] Sept. at 8 p.m.

[... &] Thurs. 1 at 2.30 p.m.

tickets

[fr]om fringe box office — 39 George Street, [... at] the door . . . . 4/- & 5/-

[...] show in town"

Sir Francis Bacon — "Sunday Tymes" 1610

Idri[s]

Entertains at the Pia[no]

"Idris Evans who has recently had su[ccessful] tours of the United States of [America,] The British West Indies. Europe a[nd ...] Africa, is worth going a long way [to see]"

Peter Noble. "Whats on i[n ...]"

Lighter side: ask anyone who has seen and heard his memorable performances with the Oxford Revues of 1957/58 during the Edinburgh Festival. Has just returned from America with recording and television contracts.

DUDLEY MOORE

at the piano

---

the press said...

1957

THE SCOTSMAN
NEWS CHRONICLE
DAILY EXPRESS
DAILY MAIL
TIMES EDUCATIONAL SUPPLEMENT

HAMLET

"Memorable and intense".

"Not to be missed".

"The best at the Festival".

"Electrically alive".

"Moved one to the quick".

Fringe programmes from 1956 to 1966

Royal Scottish Country Dance Society (Edinburgh Branch)

presents

AN EDINBURGH FANCY
1959

21st to 29th AUGUST

SCOTTISH COUNTRY DANCERS

Verse Speakers
META FORREST   IAN GILMOUR

Tenor   *Piper*
DUNCAN ROBERTSON   WILLIAM CLE...

THE COUNTRY DANCE PLAY...

THE ROYAL HIGH SCHOO...
Regent Road, Edinburgh

at 8 p.m. on

FRIDAY 21st, and SATURDAY 22nd,
and MONDAY 24th to SATURDAY 29th,
Matinees at 2...

5/-
...P. 57 G...

ADMISSION 8d.

PIANO RECITAL
by
SHEILA LESSELLS

St. Cecilia's Hall, Edinburgh

TUESDAY, 8th SEPTEMBER, 1959

at 7-30 p.m.

TICKETS   -   -   5/-, & 3/6

FRINGE SOCIETY
FFS
FESTIVAL SOCIETY
EDINBURGH

SCO... LYCEUM GALLERY
11 ATHOLL CRESCENT, EDINBURGH
16th JULY to 12th SEPTEMBER 1959

Exhibition . . . and Sale of Crafts

including:
SILVERWORK, JEWELLERY, ENGRAVED
GLASS, WROUGHT-IRON, LEATHERWORK,
HANDWOVEN TWEEDS, SCARVES, HEAD-
SQUARES and RUGS, EMBROIDERY,
HANDTHROWN POTTERY, HAND PAINTED
CHINA, BASKETRY, etc.

Open: 10 a.m.   Closing: 5 p.m. until 22nd August
and 7 p.m. from 24th
August to 12th September

CAR PARK OPPOSITE

EDINBURGH
F
F
S
FESTIVAL FRINGE SOCIETY
1966

...ial Entertainments 1956
...STIVAL City

Pringle of Scotland
CREATORS OF THE FINEST CASHMERE KNITWEAR
...OBERT PRINGLE & SON LTD., RODONO MILLS, HAWICK

The suggestion that the Fringe should become part of the official Festival was made in stronger and more particular terms. A cash subsidy was requested by a group of companies and turned down, and Hunter was asked to create an annual award to be given to the best Fringe production. This too was rejected as were the appeals to mention the Fringe shows in the Festival programme, concessionary rates for the Festival Club and invitations to Festival functions. *The Scottish Daily Express* carried a photo of a scantily-clad actress who was performing in the 1953 London Club Theatre Group's revue. The reaction of Ian Hunter to this helps to explain the Festival Society's unsympathetic attitude:

> When I see these 'sexy sketches' of the Fringe in the newspapers this morning, it is a little bit discouraging. While I have anything to do with the Festival, we will keep to the articles of association to present the very highest art. If certain sections think this is stuffy, then there it is.

The Festival's position was clear. The Fringe was too risky and risqué to be absorbed into the official programme. The unofficial groups were out on their own to stand or fall by their own endeavours. *The Scotsman* leader page observed:

> Indeed the Fringe plays a valuable part in the Edinburgh Festival. Its lack of responsibility to authority gives it a latitude which within reason allows it to experiment.

By 19 August 1952, the Society's policy-making body, the Festival Council, had come to a formal decision refusing to incorporate the Fringe. Several 'independents', said *The Scotsman*, would have refused to come under the official banner in any event, they preferred to continue along separate lines to develop something distinct from the Festival's aims.

 # Performances 1947 to 1955

Students played a catalytic part in building the Fringe's reputation for pioneering new or little-performed work. 1951 saw Edinburgh University Dramatic Society do *The Spanish Tragedy* by Thomas Kyd. This was its first performance for many years and it met with universal critical approval. *The Scotsman* took the adventurousness of the Fringe as a handy stick to beat the Festival for its conservative tastes in drama:

> *The Gentle Shepherd* and *Bartholomew Fair* certainly broke new ground but since then we have hardly had anything else comparable. Among the Shakespearean plays there have been no unusual revivals ... The Fringe, however, has given us *Philotus*, *The Flying Doctor*, *The Dog Beneath the Skin*, *The Tricks of Scapin*, *Miss Julie*, *Ralph Roister Doister*, *The Trojan Women*, *The Spanish Tragedy*, *Lysistrata* and other plays not normally seen. And in this respect the Festival authorities can hardly be said to have taken the hint.

All that by 1954 and the writer doesn't even mention the premieres.

The university groups could also enhance a production with some new ideas in staging. At Riddles Court in the Lawnmarket, the Oxford and Cambridge University Players (they later renamed themselves the Oxford Theatre Group) presented *The Taming of the Shrew* in 1952. *The Evening News* of 28 August wrote:

> The Oxford and Cambridge Players are to be congratulated on a magnificent production both as to the quality of performance and the novelty of treatment. In their comparatively small hall, with a seating capacity of not more than 150 they gave us Shakespeare in the intimate manner of the Elizabethan theatre.

The Oxford Theatre Group in *The Taming of the Shrew* **at Riddles Court in 1952**

Edinburgh University Drama Society in a scene from *The Spanish Tragedy***, 1952**

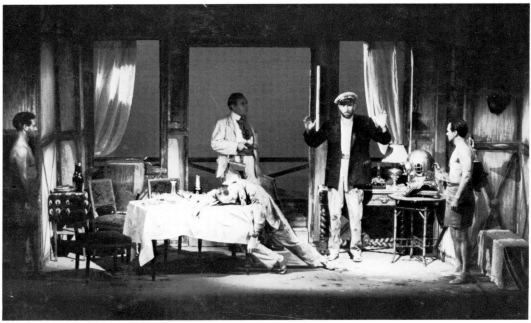

A scene from *Ebb Tide* **presented at the 1952 Fringe by the London Club Theatre Group. Donald Pleasance plays dead**

A small proscenium arch was built against one of the walls and a few chairs and an occasional table on the floor of the hall served as props. Seats were placed in front and on either side of this stage, the players being, as it were, in the midst of their audience. This merry romp took on a new glow in this friendly atmosphere and was like a gay elaborate drawing-room charade.

The practice of working and living together (as Oxford did) gave rise to a new sort of idealism which grew out of the Fringe—and later motivated the Fringe touring companies who have the craft to perform in any sort of space and who know each other well enough to create a play rather than simply perform it. The producer of the Oxford Theatre Group outlined his view of the value of the Fringe to *The Scotsman* on 10 September 1955:

Although the Oxford Theatre Group may not perform again in their tiny theatre at Riddles Court, they will leave with what, in the eyes of their producer Patrick Dromgoole, may well be a contribution to the English theatre. He described this contribution as 'a unified style which we have accidentally come across through living and working together at Riddles Court'. Because English acting had never recovered from the degenerate theatre of the nineteenth century—and could not compare with the French and other Continental theatres—there was going to be an attempt, based on the lessons learned by amateurs at Riddles Court, to work out a new and distinctive style of English theatre.

Mr Dromgoole hopes to be one of a number of people who are to form a company in London to start this attempt. Over a period of years they hope to work out this new style of English theatre and they will live, eat and work together under circumstances as similar as possible to those at Riddles Court.

Leaving aside the polemic it is clear that in the minds of performers that 'Fringe theatre' had taken on a separate meaning.

Other amateur groups could also be imaginative in compiling their Fringe programme. The Scottish Community Drama Association was a large and powerful organisation at this time and they could afford to bring foreign groups to the Little Theatre in the Pleasance. Amateur companies from Ottawa, Oslo and Rennes all performed in 1949 and 1950.

The professional contribution to the early Fringes was important for two reasons: first the companies set high standards and second, they brought in audiences who developed an early loyalty to the Fringe. The London Club Theatre Group were the most regular visitors during this period and they were occasionally joined by the Pilgrim Players from the Mercury Theatre in London, the Fraser Neal Players, the Wilson Barrett Company, the Gateway Company and several other groups got together for their Fringe productions only.

One of the most memorable of the London Club Theatre Group's many productions was Donald Pleasance's dramatisation of Robert Louis Stevenson's book, *Ebb Tide*. Here, at length, is *The Scotsman*'s review of 20 August 1952:

> There are some minor shades of difference earlier in the evening, for it is one of the tenets of this group whose policy is to produce new and unusual plays, that these plays shall be shaped in rehearsal, with the author supervising. 'Ebb Tide' is not in the strict sense a new play but it is certainly an unusual one at a time when quite three fourths of our current playwriting consists of family comedies of the conventional type. Here we are back to something like the old-fashioned melodrama, or, if that is putting it too strongly (for some of Stevenson's dialogue has a genuinely moving ring about it) then we are at any rate back to a technique which does not permit an actor to whisper or to mumble but requires a rhetorical and clear-cut speech.
>
> There is little doubt that the production methods of the group have paid a dividend. Too often the adapted play has a stiffness which betrays its source. Mr Pleasance's version of a tale in which Stevenson and Lloyd Osborne conceived three of the unpleasantest characters that novelist ever created has found convincing dramatic shape. We implicitly believe (while we see them) in Herrick, the ex-Oxfordian adrift in the world, in the Cockney Huish, and in Captain John Davis of the Searanger—the Yankee skipper whose Irish origin Michael Golden has emphasised. David Markham never lets us forget Herrick's birth, and there is a tense scene between him and Huish—the rat-faced Cockney whose sly devilry Mr Pleasance so admirably portrays—in which all Huish's hatred of gentle breeding leaps into flame. This is only excelled by the scene in which Attwater, the ruler of the uncharted island, plies Huish with drink for information—a scene which Mr Pleasance has finely imagined.
>
> If there is one part more than another which should induce visitors to seek out this unofficial contribution to the Festival, then it is certainly Willoughby Goddard's picturesque Attwater. Mr Goddard's conception of this megalomaniac and religious fanatic is on the grand scale, and it is superbly done. How admirable is his contempt conveyed in the mere mispronunciation of his name!
>
> The evening is not all stark horror. There is humour too, and the way in which the discovery is made that the Farralone's cargo is worthless is one of the most rewarding moments of all. Peter Streuli's production is magnificent make-believe, which preserves the full quality of Stevenson's colourful yarn.

Looking at the period from 1947 to 1955 as a whole, it is surprising how easily accepted the early Fringe groups were, and how much co-operation from the authorities they received. For example, Edinburgh University Drama Society were allowed to use the Students' Common Room in the Old College (out of term time) by the Secretary,

Charles Stewart. They were allowed to sleep there on beds which the Lord Provost found for them from his Social Services Department. The City Licensing authorities gave help in showing groups how to remain within the safety regulations. Critics were usually kind and considerate of the difficulties Fringe groups had. And finally the era of hostility between the Festival Society and the Fringe was only just beginning.

As the Fringe became more independent and more radical, it enjoyed less and less co-operation but more and more artistic freedom.

Cartoon by Michael Heath. 'The Fringe meet the Press at the Fringe Club.'
Reproduced courtesy of Punch

PART TWO

1956 TO 1959

The Development of Continuity

The Fringe programmes which had been independently speculated by Ian Cousland in 1954 began to appear regularly with the rather coy heading 'Additional Entertainments'. Evidently 'Fringe' was still considered a slang expression, all right for the newspapers but not for the performers. This coyness about words is important. Obviously the way in which people think about something is expressed in their choice of words and if attitudes change then language reflects that change. By the end of this period everyone talks about 'Fringe', and 'Additional Entertainments' has disappeared. This represented one symptom of the growing independence of the Fringe, it was no longer seen as merely an 'Additional' facet of the Edinburgh Festival. People had come to expect something of the Fringe, as a permanent feature.

Cousland's programmes give a much clearer idea of the collective development of the Fringe in the late Fifties, and by the end of the period they contain virtually all the groups performing in Edinburgh at Festival time but who are not included in the official programme. The traditional distinctions within the Fringe between amateurs, students and professionals are seen to be changing significantly; in 1955 there were three purely amateur groups rising to eight by 1959. The numbers of professionals fluctuated hardly at all but the nature of their shows began to change. The large companies like the Wilson Barrett Company, the Gateway Company and Duncan MacRae's Scottishshows group were not so prominent and the small one or two-hander shows became more popular. Sonia Dresdel, Donald Wolfit and Elspeth Douglas-Reid pioneered these in Edinburgh and they were followed by more professionals anxious to cut costs and simplify what could be a risky venture. Finally, the student element also remained fairly constant in its numbers throughout this period, with Sheffield, Cardiff and Cambridge joining Edinburgh and Oxford in 1956. The role of the students did change in its nature though: university theatre groups began to be innovative in the shows they did and the way in which they performed them.

At the same time as the content of the Fringe programme was changing, it began to grow in size. Numbers of groups rose from thirteen in 1955 to nineteen in 1959—and this total has increased steadily ever since then. This volume of entertainment, vastly more than what the Festival could offer, provided a good cross-section of the arts and began to look like an alternative festival existing to exploit the contrast with official offerings.

Innovation and the Right to Fail

With the advent of television as a mass medium, there now exists a strong temptation in the theatre to avoid risks and rely on formulae of proven success. In the main, London's theatre listings make disheartening reading with such a heavy emphasis on revivals, farces, sex shows, sex comedies, and plays which are vehicles for actors who made their reputations on television. Few new plays get performed in the West End, which is, after

A scene from *Doctor Jo* **performed by the Fraser Neal Players starring Sonia Dresdel**

The Players of Leyton with Derek Jacobi (seated) as *Hamlet*, **1958**

The Oxford Theatre Group in Willis Hall's *The Disciplines of War*, **in 1958, which later opened in London's West End as** *The Long, the Short and the Tall*

all, the area in Britain with the greatest concentration of permanent theatres. In the Fringe, in its nationwide form, the accent is almost exclusively on new plays often by untried writers. This tradition has its origins in Edinburgh with the early Fringe groups.

Both the universities which dominated the first years of the Fringe, Edinburgh and Oxford, had a clear commitment to doing new or seldom-performed work. The Oxford Theatre Group always did British or world premieres, and in this period one can grasp the breadth of their enterprise simply by listing what they did: 1956, *Storm in Shanghai* by André Malraux: 1957, *Corruption in the Palace of Justice* by Ugo Betti: 1958 *The Disciplines of War* by Willis Hall: 1959, *Why the Chicken* by John McGrath.

Edinburgh University Dramatic Society (with the help of their Graduate Theatre Group) performed *The Baikie Charivari* by James Bridie. This play was discovered in a drawer after Bridie's death and it was introduced into the repertoire through this production in 1957. The following year the same group did *The Adam Comedy* by the Capek Brothers. This is a satire on the creation myth where Adam succeeds in blowing up the world and God then asks him to try his hand at moulding clay into living things. The plot had topicality as well as originality since it was performed in the late Fifties when the CND were becoming increasingly important.

The professional companies also brought new work to Edinburgh. Most important was the London Club Theatre Group who performed regularly on the Fringe throughout the decade until 1959 when their director, Brian Bailey was killed in a car crash and the group split up. They did three premieres in succession from 1956 to 1958: *Twice Five* by Philip Guard, *The Queen and the Welshman* by Rosemary Anne Sisson, and *Rashid* by Dorothy Lang. Because these companies, both students and professionals, had built a reputation and took risks with their choice of plays, they attracted large audiences.

> The Fringe's power lies in the fact that a good group with a 'different' play can find an audience in Edinburgh—its weakness is that sometimes audiences are enthusiastic because of the newness of the plays rather than their dramatic merit.   *The Evening Dispatch* 23 August 1957

Companies were not only innovative in finding original work as the basis of their Fringe reputation but also in introducing different techniques. A student group with the forbidding name of The Sporranslitters did a show at the Braidburn Outdoor Theatre in Morningside. It was *The Puddocks* translated 'frae the Greek o' Aristophanes' by Douglas Young. That is, *The Frogs* translated into Scots. Three to four hundred stalwarts turned out to sit on the cold wooden seats to watch the spectacle. The Braid Burn had been dammed so that Dionysus could enjoy a real Styx to row across and so that the Puddocks could splash about realistically. The chorus entered bearing flaming torches to light the show; and so that speeches could be heard the principal actors harangued the shivering audience with loud-hailers. Although *The Scotsman* drama critic, Ronald Mavor, gave the show an enthusiastic review, it sounds as though he forgot to take his hip-flask. He insisted:

> The show must run for no more than 1½ hours and should run right through without an interval. It may then, given a little fine weather, take its rightful place as one of the many experiences over the past 11 years for which we must be grateful to the Festival Fringe.

The Festival Society used to hire almost all of the fully equipped theatres leaving small, often bare halls to the Fringe. For this reason circumstances often forced groups to be inventive in setting their shows. T. M. Watson commented in *The Weekly Scotsman* during the 1957 Fringe:

> Whether necessity forced the Oxford Theatre Group to use the arena stage instead of the more conventional picture frame, matters little. Within a few minutes of the lights going up on Ugo

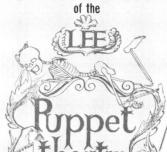

**Handbills and posters
from the early Fringe**

Betti's *Corruption in the Palace of Justice* the audience accepted the novelty and promptly forgot it. No higher compliment could be paid to the producer and his cast for there is nothing more difficult in the theatre than to get the audience to accept the unusual.

Watson seemed to regard the Oxford setting as an inconvenience overcome rather than a deliberate part of a unified style; but in his opinion some groups were unable to come to terms with their theatre-spaces. Aberdeen University did *The Eagle has Two Heads* by Jean Cocteau in St George's Church Hall, and Watson wrote in *The Weekly Scotsman* of 31 August 1957:

> A small intimate hall is all against the style of acting required for this type of play, while the part of the Queen requires a virtuoso performance of which no amateur is capable.

Some amateurs were capable of great imagination even bordering on eccentricity:

> How far does the Fringe extend? This Saturday the Wayside Players are presenting *Festival Fringe*, a programme of comedy drama and theatre ballet at Invergowrie (in the county of Angus). That is quite a step from Princes Street and I cannot see many making the trip despite the novelty offered, for the show is being presented on a garden terrace as an experiment in outdoor theatre. Outdoor theatre in Scotland richly deserves the experimental tag and Alastair T. Moffat, the originator of the idea, must be a brave man in addition to being a candid one. He says there is a wonderful view of the Tay from the terrace of his house, Carsecraig, where the show is being given, so, if the audience do not like the plays, there is always the scenery to admire.
>
> *The Weekly Scotsman* August 1957

Frequently the enterprise of Fringe groups, at least those who chose to stay in Edinburgh, showed up the continuing conservative tastes of the Festival director in the area of drama. In 1959 the playwright, Hugh Ross Williamson said in *The Scotsman*:

> Nobody in their senses would go to the official Festival. I think it is scandalous that in the three weeks of the year when Edinburgh takes precedence over London or any other place in the British Isles they must put on this old 'ham'.
>
> What I would like to see is the Edinburgh Festival reassert itself by refusing, for instance, to have the Old Vic unless the Old Vic does something new. All of the Festival drama this year is very dull.

Four years before that, the Festival Society had premiered *The Hidden King* by Jonathan Griffin and it had been savaged by the critics. And it is possible that this experience discouraged the taking of further risks. On the Fringe, on a smaller economic scale, the consequences of failure are less severe.

> Can we afford to take risks at a Festival? Risks, of course, will be taken and are taken every time with many Fringe productions and if they result in failure no-one will grumble much. But is it not different with a Festival play?

It is different with a Festival play, and there is no question that the Festival's unimaginative attitude to drama helped shift the emphasis over to the Fringe, as far as new work is concerned. Kenneth Tynan in *The Observer* during the 1959 Fringe:

> The Oxford Theatre Group is just the kind of Fringe organisation which ought to be encouraged more actively by any city preparing a Festival. At least it has commissioned a play, *Why the Chicken* by a very young and lively writer, John McGrath, whereas the Festival Society gives an impression of disinteresting itself in the theatre except as a testing ground for subsequent London productions, or a shopwindow for Scottish repertory companies.

Frequently groups found that freshness and inventiveness were, in the late Fifties, no more foolproof ingredients for a successful show than they are today. For example, when the Oxford Arena Theatre arrived in Edinburgh in 1958 and took over the Sandeman Hall behind John Knox's House in the High Street, it produced a smart programme using sponsorship from a private company, and their shows promised much: Ionesco's *The Picture* and Arthur Adamov's *The Invasion* in 'an experimental double bill from the Parisian avant-garde' and Pirandello's *It's Only a Joke* in the late-night slot. The Ionesco production dazzled the critic from the *Evening News*:

> Since the advent of T.V., the theatre has been searching for something to hold its appeal and restore its former glory. One of the most successful 'innovations' has been theatre-in-the-round, whereby the audience is on all sides of the players, creating greater intimacy and naturalism. This technique has been adopted in two 'avant-garde' plays with great success by the oxford Arena Theatre. The specially constructed set for *The Picture*, a structure rather like contemporary wrought-iron work, is of great assistance in maintaining the surrealistic atmosphere of the play, which, although of an essentially extrovert nature has several facets of non-representational theatre.

All the other critics felt that the show was completely non-representational—in fact, completely disastrous. But these extracts give a better picture than the bad reviews of what the students were aiming at and how they failed. The same critic was less clear about the Adamov play:

> Being given its British premiere last night was Adamov's *The Invasion*, an exercise in symbolism, which, although possessive of intense atmosphere and feeling for character, is somehow too vague in its message to register on the conventional British mind.
>
> Undoubtedly Adamov provides an interesting experiment in technique and his first translation of his work in English provides some moving dialogue, but his work being almost in its entirety non-representational requires closer scrutiny before a decision can be finalised.

Sadly for them, audiences were not forthcoming at the Oxford Arena Theatre's productions but they struggled bravely to the end of the Festival, affirming the right of all Fringe groups to fail. That right seemed to be slipping away from Festival-sponsored productions.

The Late Night Revues

Revue has always been seen as a cardinal feature of the Fringe. In a festival set-up late night entertainment is in demand, especially from those seeking light relief after an ennervating evening at the Usher Hall. The Fringe was not long in identifying this demand with both student and professional groups mounting late shows. The first revue at the Edinburgh Festival seems to have been in the 1952 Fringe when the New Drama Group did a series of sketches called *After the Show*, the show being Donald Pleasance's *Ebb Tide*. It was written by Peter Myers and Alec Grahame, starring Betty Marsden and Eunice Gayson. This was a London production transferred *en bloc* to cash in on the wide-open market for late shows at the Edinburgh Festival. The next year two revues appeared; the London Theatre Club Group's offering nearly wasn't Fringe according to *The Scotsman* report:

> It follows the highly successful introduction last year during the Festival season by this Fringe

organisation of a late night show under the title 'After the Show'. This year's revue 'See You Later' was actually offered to Mr Hunter (the Festival Director) in London for official Festival acceptance, but nothing came of it, and the London Theatre Group brought the show to the city on their own responsibility.

See You Later was written by Sandy Wilson and starred Duncan MacRae and Fenella Fielding. It was enormously popular and slightly risqué. Several prominent individuals, including Mr Hunter, complained that it was smutty and *The Scotsman* reviewer was mildly disapproving of 'scantily clad young ladies', but, like most of his fellow citizens, he did not allow that to impair his enjoyment of the show.

The London Theatre Club Group's revue filled the Palladium Theatre each night of its run, not suffering at all from competition from the Oxford Theatre Group's *Cakes and Ale* which was the first of many university revues to come to Edinburgh. The audience for late shows was so large that both did much more than survive. Incidentally Miss Margaret Smith began a long succession of good notices with her performance in *Cakes and Ale*. No-one accused the students of using risqué gags and Miss Smith did not appear 'scantily-clad'. That long tradition was begun by professionals, in a series of shows at the Palladium, although to this day students have been seen as the chief purveyors of outrage and indecency.

R. H. Westwater, the arts critic of the now sadly defunct *Weekly Scotsman* liked to refer to the Fringe as the lighter side of the Festival. He was in the habit of telling his readers, in some detail, what he planned to see during the Festival. As a supporter of the official events, most of what he saw on the Fringe was late-night, that is, revue. The same was true of many of the reviewers who only came up from London for two or three days. In this way

Reproduced courtesy of Scotsman Publications
Donald Wolfit in *The Strong Are Lonely,* **1956**

the Fringe was seen as being, at least until the mid-Sixties, largely about revues and mainly student ones at that. This is a false impression—although it must be admitted that the revue, *Beyond the Fringe* (which was actually in the 1960 Festival programme) probably did more to broadcast the name of 'Fringe' than anything else at the time.

By 1955 the students had come to be regarded as superior to the professionals in the field of revue. *The Scotsman* drama critic wrote:

> The pattern for (professional) Festival revues has become, even in the short space of three years, firmly set. There is the backbone of West End skits and sketches interspersed with Scottish or Festival items.

In contrast the university revues were original, and written especially for the Fringe by talented young writers like Ned Sherrin, who made an impact with critics in 1955. In 1958 Ken Loach and Dudley Moore appeared in the Oxford Theatre Group's *Just Lately* at the Cranston Street Hall. The following year Moore, starting out on his professional career, turned up with Frederick Fuller, a concert baritone, to perform in the Gartshore Hall in George Street. He accompanied Fuller on the piano. The Oxford Revue that year included Alan Bennett and Giles Havergal in *Better Never*.

Many other highly successful performers first made a critical success on the Edinburgh Fringe, but it would be fatuous to claim that the Fringe 'made' anyone's career. All it did, and does, was provide a platform for anyone who, if they are good enough, can enjoy national, and even international, critical and popular acclaim. Anna Quayle, for example, was unknown when she was praised for her performances in the 1956 Oxford revue: 'a girl with the comic qualities of Joyce Grenfell—was perhaps the most outstanding'. Such encouragement must have helped to establish her confidence and prompted her to think of the stage as a career.

 # The Fringe as Counter-Festival

Donald Wolfit's *The Strong Are Lonely* from the 1956 Fringe was not only popular but considered to be of 'Festival standard'. Many people argued that the show should have been included in the official programme. It didn't seem to matter to Wolfit.

> Donald Wolfit knew nothing whatever 'about this thing called the Fringe'. He declared: 'Away with the Fringe. To an artist in the theatre there is no such thing as a fringe of art. Wherever an artist is, there is the centre of his art. The citizens of Edinburgh are ratepayers and contribute to the Festival and if public buildings are to be used as part of the regular theatres then these should be properly recognised and given a place in the programme.

Attitudes had changed by 1959 when Duncan MacRae spoke to members of the Fringe Club:

> Only within the Fringe itself was one likely to find any modern work of art at all, anything virile and youthful, the Scottish actor Duncan MacRae said in Edinburgh yesterday.
> 'The Festival Society', he explained, 'must have certain criteria in the choice of orchestras, operas and dramas. Their choice must be in accord with criteria which a large number of people will accept.' This meant that at the very moment of their judging what was to be in, they were already out of date. 'There can be no criterion for what is new', he said. 'Only old things can be compared and reach the academic standard by which the Festival Society is bound to abide.' Mr MacRae said he did not think the Fringe need change a great deal. He spoke of the problem of

The *Beyond the Fringe* **team, Peter Cook, Dudley Moore, Alan Bennett and Jonathan Miller appearing at the official Festival in 1960**

finding accommodation for Fringe productions and said that all over the country companies and local authorities were building fine theatres for social and welfare purposes. But these 'lacked atmosphere'. What he enjoyed about Fringe groups who found themselves 'a little rathole down behind the Castle' was that their halls had a warmth which was lacking in newer and much larger halls.

In 1956 Wolfit had refused to recognise the existence of the Fringe despite the fact that he found himself on it, and by 1959 Duncan MacRae is defining what the Fringe is about and listing its merits. In the time between these statements the Fringe had come to mean something very different from the Festival.

Not only were new plays done but all the arts came to be represented in the Fringe programme. There had always been many visual arts exhibitions all over the city at Festival time. The commercial galleries, such as Aitken Dott in Castle Street, had mounted selling exhibitions ever since 1947, and professional artists had occasionally put on one-man shows. The Saltire Society had begun to organise poetry readings, recitals and exhibitions which allowed visitors to see a bit more deeply into Scotland's culture than was possible through the tartanned windows of the High Street gift shops. Fringe music, like Fringe drama, could be innovative. Sandy Thomas Ross wrote a folk opera in Scots which he called *Tod Lowrie* (a Scots name for a fox). It was premiered in 1956 at the Central Halls, Tollcross and it attracted puzzled critical attention. Thea Musgrave's *Divertimento for Strings, Opus 15* was premiered in Gladstone's Land, the headquarters of the Saltire Society, in the Lawnmarket. In addition small ensembles of local musicians gave concerts and the Royal Scottish Country Dance Society began their popular series,

An Edinburgh Fancy, in the hall of the Royal High School. The music category of the Fringe programme has become a strong one but it is, curiously, underestimated.

By the end of the Fifties the Fringe programme could provide a complete alternative to the official Festival—a counter-festival programme in fact. But it needed to be better organised before it could reach its public efficiently.

The Formation of the Fringe Society

From its earliest years the Fringe had been encouraged to form itself into a coherent organisation, or become attached to the Festival Society in some way. In reality the Festival could hardly have run a pet Fringe without making it a junior branch of the official event with invited groups of whom something would naturally be expected, and it had rightly rejected the idea. The Fringe was forced into looking after itself. This began with the publication of the early programmes and the establishment of the central box office run by Edinburgh University students. Not all groups used these early services, either through choice or ignorance, but gradually it became essential to be included. If a group was not included then many people got the impression that they had not appeared that year. for example the 1956 Fringe programme did not carry the details of Donald Wolfit's show *The Strong Are Lonely* which ran for three weeks at the Lauriston Hall. Because of Wolfit's reputation and the play's already good press, it did well. But the After Dinner Opera Company from the United States were badly attended in the same year because they were not a big name, and more importantly, had been left out of the Fringe programme. By 1959 not even well known groups dared to risk being left out.

The programmes and the box office together gave a corporate identity to the Fringe which was cemented by the formation of a Fringe Society. It was only a matter of time before this came about and it fell to the Oxford Theatre Group's director, Michael Imison, to take the initiative. He called a meeting of Fringe groups for 29 August at the Cranston Street Hall in the Canongate. Attendance was poor, with only eight groups turning up. The likely reason for this was that Michael Imison had misjudged the temper of the Fringe. *The Scotsman* reported on 30 August:

> A suggestion by Mr Imison that the proposed society should attempt to gain recognition by the Festival Society did not go down well with the other delegates. 'We don't want recognition' was the general consensus of opinion.
>
> 'But why do we want to be recognised by the official Festival Society?' asked Mr Piers Haggard, president of Edinburgh University Dramatic Society. 'Recognition would bring ties. And we could so easily get swallowed up in the big machine that works in George Street and the Usher Hall.'

Through a curious slip-up in distributing invitations to the meeting, no professional companies attended, but they nevertheless supported the idea of forming a Fringe Society. Charles Baptiste of the Rutherglen Repertory Company spoke to *The Scotsman* of 8 September:

> 'Whether you are amateur, semi-professional or professional, it is a question of putting on something worthwhile, of putting on a high standard of production and performance which will be accepted by a high standard of audience. To do that,' he went on, 'you require co-ordination behind it.'

By the end of the 1958 Festival, Fringe Society office bearers had been elected and a list of aims had been drawn up. All groups who planned to appear on the Fringe in 1959 were asked to contact Ian Cousland, the Society's secretary. The intention was to publish a complete programme of all the events not in the official Festival programme, maintain an information bureau and run a club, and a central box office to sell all groups' tickets.

As a direct result of the wishes of the participants, the Society had been set up to help the performers who came to Edinburgh and to promote them collectively to the public. They did not come together so that groups could be vetted or invited or in some way controlled artistically. What was performed and how it was done was left entirely up to each Fringe group. Essentially that is how the Fringe Society operates today.

Cartoon by Michael Heath at the 1977 Fringe 'Don't worry about me, lads—I'm suffering from review lag.'

Reproduced courtesy of Punch

PART THREE

1960

TO

1969

The Structure of the Fringe Society

By 1960 the Festival Fringe Society had developed a simple structure to cope with the needs of the groups and the demands of their public. Its first president was Michael Imison from the Oxford Theatre Group: the man who had made the initial moves to set up the Society in 1958. The General Secretary was Ian Cousland, the printer who had speculated the first programmes.

One of the major functions of the new Society was to keep the public well informed about the activities of Fringe Groups. The main medium for doing this was the Fringe Programme. This extended from 24 to 32 pages depending on the number of groups participating. Each group was asked to submit its programme details for inclusion, if they intended to join the Fringe Society. The membership subscription in 1961 was £10 for a group returning to Edinburgh and £11 for a newcomer. This amount of money was intended to cover expenses in running the Fringe Society but it came to represent the cost of being included in the Fringe Programme.

The early programmes carried much advertising which acted as a useful source of revenue and, until a bad debt cropped up from the programme's space seller, it paid for printing costs. The distribution of the programme at that time was limited to Edinburgh and parts of Scotland. It was also sent out on request to potential visitors to the Festival.

Despite the fact that not all groups came into it, the readily available and generally correct Fringe programmes stand as one of the important achievements of the Fringe Society and its voluntary officers.

The Festival Club had existed from the beginning as a centre for artists and the public to gather and eat and drink at all hours of the day. In this way it acted as a social focus for the official Festival. The new Fringe Society decided to create something similar for their members and the public. In 1959, the Fringe Club opened at the YMCA in South St Andrew Street. It ran from 10.00 am until 11.30 pm each day and provided meals and coffee or soft drinks. For most of the club's stay at the YMCA, the Association's temperant influence prevented the sale of anything more intoxicating. Membership was 10/6d for three weeks—which seems now to be expensive in view of the fact that the facilities comprised only 'a spacious lounge', and a series of morning lectures by visiting celebrities. Nevertheless the Club did help to mark out the differences between official and Fringe— and on a basic level provided the groups with somewhere to go or foregather.

Also in the YMCA was the Fringe box office, which held tickets for almost all groups. Although shops like the Edinburgh Bookshop and Rae Macintosh sold tickets for the Fringe, the YMCA had the most comprehensive choice. The Society charged a commission of 5% on all sales. This was used to pay staff—people like Mrs Alice Tulloch who worked in the original box office at the YMCA and now runs the huge operation at 170 High Street.

Allied to the selling of tickets was the Information Bureau. Its very important function was to help the public pick their way through the programme and its oddities. But, it needs to be stressed that no group ever received a recommendation from any of the Fringe staff. The most frequent question from the public still is 'What's the best show you have?' The answer always is 'Look at the newspaper reviews, we never promote one show above another'. The nature of the democracy of the Fringe is important and is central to the nature of the Fringe itself.

Returning to the early Fringe Society, there were two vital jobs to be done for groups before they arrived in Edinburgh. The first was to warn those considering appearing on the Fringe that it was not easy, nor was it likely to be profitable, at least in cash terms. Jim Gallacher, the first Publicity Secretary, wrote a leaflet which explained how the Fringe Society worked. He called it 'Fringe Without Tears' and in it he listed the pitfalls and problems. Competition was tough, he warned, not only from other Fringe groups but also from the official offerings, including the Film Festival (which had started in 1947) and the Military Tattoo. The practicalities of hiring a suitable hall were outlined as were the procedures for obtaining a Public Entertainment Licence. Publicity, the Press, ticket-printing and posters were all extensively discussed and it was made clear that all of these were the responsibility of the performing groups. The Fringe Society existed to provide advice and information and central services at Festival time.

The second important job undertaken by the Society was the publication of bi-monthly bulletins. These were posted to groups and attempted to anticipate queries about the mechanics of coming to perform on the Edinburgh Fringe. Reminders to check your hall-rental, get a licence from the Lord Chamberlain, find cheap accommodation were all part of an educational process which helped the groups to be successful in Edinburgh, and also to inform their members who branched out into the professional Fringe companies in the late Sixties. It is difficult to trace the influence of the Fringe in this direction, other than in very general terms. A touring company which uses pure Edinburgh Fringe techniques, however, is the 7:84 Theatre Company (see page 89).

The finances of the Fringe Society in the Sixties were not unhealthy. Most years a small surplus was realised and the accumulated reserves were invested and the revenue therefrom being used to improve services to the groups and the public. This was possible because the groups did so much for themselves—and still do: the one financially unsuccessful year, 1966, was the result of a drop in the Society's membership.

The stability of the Fringe's finances was also the result of the efforts by the Society's administrators, a group of volunteers who were prepared to shoulder responsibility and devote time and effort to the job. There were four main officers—the President, the General Secretary, the Publicity Secretary and the Treasurer. Janet Lewis and Liz Willis both developed an interest in the Fringe through being active in an Edinburgh amateur group and once their energies had transferred to the Society itself, both women gave long and much-appreciated services during the Sixties. Patrick Brooks had also been involved with an amateur company, Edinburgh University Drama Society. He became Treasurer of the Fringe in 1964, President in 1969 and finally severed his association with the Society in 1972. Brooks identified strongly with the aspirations of the Fringe and was energetic in seeking recognition from all quarters; the City, the Arts Council, the official Festival. His long service gave a continuity and a depth of experience which was unusual in the Arts at that time. The generosity of service of Patrick Brooks and his colleagues ought to be more widely recognised than it is. The Fringe would never have struggled out from under the Festival without their help.

The committee of management of the Fringe Society was supplemented by representatives of the Fringe groups. This happened from the beginning so that the policy of the Fringe could derive directly from those who used it and needed it. This practice prevented the Society from drifting from its role as a giver of advice and information. It could have become an ordinary promoting festival which made up its programme by inviting groups. It remained as an open festival because it was directed by those who had taken advantage of its openness by coming to perform in Edinburgh.

Performances 1960 to 1962

One of the most consistent claims of the Fringe Society was that their Programme offered a far greater diversity of entertainment than the official Festival. This was certainly true by the early Sixties when puppets, revue, serious drama, musical and poetry recitals, exhibitions, miracle plays and comedies could all be enjoyed, or not. The other form of diversity to be found was a great unevenness in the quality of productions. As fewer professional groups came, and more universities, the overall standard seems, on balance, to have declined. Critics were not anxious to be unkind—here, for example, is a review of Sheffield University Drama Group's *The Lunatic View* by David Campton:

> The Sheffield Group were good and bad in this play. When they were bad they were terrible but when they were good they were pleasing. Yorkshire grit saw them through. Practice will polish them. Well tried.

Although that review sounds condescending in the extreme, it seems unlikely that it was intended to be. Critics were used to giving groups encouragement and were usually mindful of their amateur status. When numbers of groups participating rose dramatically in the late Sixties and again in the mid-Seventies, the competition of so much that was good with so much that was bad made critics less generous.

Controversy as well as quality attracted attention. Ric Throssell's play *The Day Before Tomorrow* was performed by the London Playgoers Club in a hall in Hill Street. It was about the aftermath of an atomic explosion and the difficulties of survival in a devastated world. The CND was at its height during this period and the play helped people to grasp the dangers of nuclear weapons more readily. Several excellent performances and some good writing made *The Day Before Tomorrow* one of the highlights of the 1960 Fringe.

The same year saw the engaging headline to a Fringe review 'Audience of 20 Numbed'. This began a devastatingly bad review of Bill Owen's *Fringe of Light,* an Osbornesque domestic drama. The script was seized by the police and examined before the show was allowed to go on. The critic who reviewed it thought it a misjudgement on the part of the police to return it:

> The plot is wearisome and abstruse; centring on the vapourings of Sara, a young girl, whose author husband has run off with a woman publisher. Characters keep rushing on and off stage; doors slam, voices screech. It is all very confusing.

Despite this, he goes on to say how he liked some of the performances.

Premiere productions were very much to the fore in this period. Tom Wright wrote *The Mask* for Glasgow's College of Dramatic Arts. He later went on to write *There Was A Man,* a much-travelled one-man show on Burns, played by John Cairney. The Oxford Theatre Group continued its tradition of doing new work with *Vasco* in 1960, and *Songs For An Autumn Rifle* in 1961. This last, by David Caute, was about a Hungarian newspaper editor during the 1956 uprising. It went on in tandem with the Oxford Revue which starred, amongst others, John Wells, Giles Havergal, William Rushton and Richard Ingrams. In 1963, Oxford introduced an unfamiliar work of Arthur Adamov to British audiences with their production of *Paolo Paoli.*

Cambridge University Theatre Company was formed in 1962 with the sole purpose of bringing shows to the Edinburgh Fringe. It incorporated the Footlights revue with a programme of serious plays—one of which, *Brand* by Henrik Ibsen, was directed by

Trevor Nunn. Although it received very good notices, the CUTC have brought only the Footlights to Edinburgh on anything like a regular basis. Other universities began to be successful and in 1961 the 60 Theatre Group from London University scored a notable success with their production of *The Seven Who Were Hanged* by Leonid Andreyev:

> It is about five young revolutionaries who are hanged, along with two more deserving felons, at the end of the play. As presented at the Royal Arch Hall by the 60 Theatre Group, it is a moving and a cheering experience and an example of how very good performances can be on the Fringe.

> Ronald Mavor, *The Scotsman*

The East London Theatre Group also brought new work to Edinburgh in the early Sixties. *The Philosophy of Joseph Grind, Nocturne From Hellespont* and *Hoax* were three short plays by Albert Jeanes performed by a company who publicised themselves under the banner 'Dockland Comes to Lochland'. Although professional Scottish companies appeared much less frequently in this period than in the Fifties, the Mercat Theatre Trust (a Church of Scotland foundation) presented two plays at the Lauriston Hall in 1961 and 1962. Their first production was a new play by Maurice McLoughlin, *A Letter From The General*, starring Lennox Milne and directed by Gerard Slevin. Although the show was not badly reviewed and it seems unlikely that it was badly attended, Slevin launched an extraordinary attack on the Fringe Society. He claimed that the Fringe was too big and that people presenting 'intellectual' plays should be discouraged:

> I think there should be a limitation on the number of halls used during the Festival. It would be much better if only ten halls were licensed. These could very well be balloted for and everyone would be much happier.

This outburst probably articulated a resentment against unwelcome competition which some professionals felt. The remarks about 'intellectual' plays could easily be seen as an attack on the growing student element in the Fringe. Even though it is very far from the truth, for a long time it remained part of the conventional theatrical wisdom that the Fringe was really only for amateurs and students. Despite his feelings about the Fringe in 1961, Gerard Slevin returned the following year to do a second Mercat production, *No Man's Boat* by Alejandro Casona, starring Paul Kermack and Madeleine Christie.

Rather than complaining about the nature of the Fringe, two groups of people in particular took advantage of its openness to publicise their activities.

In Victoria Street, on the site of what is now Nicky Tams, a jazz/folk club called The Place was started. At Festival time they brought big names to Edinburgh: Memphis Slim, Chris Barber, Champion Jack Dupree. By introducing another side to the Fringe, The Place was able to exploit the Festival in the same way that the early Fringe groups had done.

John Calder, a publisher, organised an International Writers Conference in the McEwen Hall. He invited an impressive list of names including Hugh MacDiarmid whose seventieth birthday fell in 1962. Calder's conference honoured MacDiarmid, while the official Festival failed to notice the event. In 1963 an official International Drama Conference was promoted by Calder. This was chaired by Kenneth Tynan and again many famous names attended: Arthur Adamov, Arnold Wesker, Max Frisch and Edward Albee amongst many others. Incidentally this was the famous occasion when a naked lady was wheeled into the proceedings, apparently in an effort to liven up what was becoming a rather dull affair.

Coming back to the Fringe itself, the years 1960 to 1962 can be seen as the period when the student contribution became more definite. The professional companies began to fade out—although small-scale enterprises like one- or two-hander shows were always in evidence. It was also the period when relations with the official Festival were at their worst.

Competitor or Complement— Relations with the official Festival

Jim Gallacher's leaflet, *Fringe Without Tears*, contained all sorts of advice for groups. One of the most prominent warnings was about the Festival Society:

> Festival vs Fringe. Do not expect much help from the official Festival Society. As a body it resolutely refuses to recognise its 'poor relations', but despite this, its individual officers are as co-operative as their duties will allow—in any case there is no harm in asking!

The Edinburgh International Festival's policy making body is the Festival Council, and opposition to the Fringe used to stem from there. In the late Fifties it was strongly argued in the Council that any other attractions in Edinburgh at Festival time represented a threat to the official box-office, and that therefore, these events ought to be discouraged. As Gallacher's leaflet implies, the paid executives generally found this attitude to be a short-sighted one and, unofficially, did as much as they could to help.

The major manifestation of this coolness between the Fringe and the Festival was the continued omission of the merest mention of the Fringe in any of the official publications. Obviously the public was interested in both, and the Festival Society had it in its power to boost Fringe audiences greatly by giving visitors foreknowledge of its existence. Repeated appeals were made by the Fringe Society but each time the Festival Council rejected them. Lack of space in a 100-page Souvenir Brochure was given as one excuse. The possibility that Fringe productions would be of such a low standard that the Festival Society could not be associated with them—this was once offered as another excuse. So it ground on until the advent of Peter Diamand. He attended the opening party for the Fringe in 1966 and has done so each year, despite criticism from his Council. In 1967 a Fringe poster was put up in both the Festival Club and the Festival office. And in 1969 the Council at last resolved to allow a mention of the Fringe in the Festival Programme Brochure. Apart from a break in 1971 when the Festival Society had to reduce the size of its brochure, the Fringe has been mentioned regularly. This is of great value to the Society whose slender means do not permit the extensive publicity enjoyed by the Festival.

The early antagonism made itself evident in niggling ways. For example, when the Fringe Club started to mount their celebrity coffee mornings, the Festival Council refused to allow their artists to participate. More, they considered setting up a rival club for young Festival visitors. And finally a comical episode when a Fringe group, the Edinburgh Graduate Theatre Group, did a spoof on the official logo. They were ordered to withdraw all their publicity on pain of legal action. They did not withdraw, and were not actually prosecuted, but the upshot of it all was the spectacle of a somewhat humourless Festival Society.

And yet in spite of this bureaucratic cold war, there existed a healthy element of artistic co-operation between the two organisations. The Fringe could act as a try-out festival for shows which might, at some future time, be included in the official programme. The famous revue *Beyond the Fringe* was the first in a succession of transfers of ideas and talent. The Traverse Theatre itself set up Traverse Festival Productions and did the official *Macbeth* in 1965 at the Assembly Halls. And in 1967 Peter Diamand showed his admiration for the work of Fringe companies by including three in his drama programme. The Traverse mounted a production of Paul Foster's *Tom Paine* at the Church Hill Theatre. This was really the La Mama Troupe from New York who had performed on the Fringe a year previously. The Traverse's equivalent in Glasgow, the Close Theatre, did three short plays by Olwen Wymark, collectively entitled *Triple Image*. And the Hampstead Theatre Club came north from London to do two Barry Bermange plays, *Nathan and Tabileth*, and *Oldenberg*. Perhaps the fastest transfer from Fringe to Festival was Larry Adler who took over the late night slot at the Lyceum from Elizabeth Seal whose show had been cancelled by the Festival Society after only one performance (no official reason was given). So Adler and Seal swopped over with Jim Haynes of the Traverse finding the latter a hall in the Fringe.

The Lord Provost of Edinburgh is traditionally Chairman of the Festival Council and in the Sixties he was often seen reflecting the attitudes to the Fringe of both Town Council and Festival Society. In 1964 a deputation of student groups led by Jon Silken of Durham sent a petition to the Provost calling for greater co-operation with the Festival. Not only was this rejected but the Corporation reacted by tightening up theatre licensing laws for those groups using temporary performance spaces. Although the petitions did not originate from the Fringe Society, they did represent the frustrations of many performers. At all events, a period of truce ensued until Peter Diamand took office in 1966, the date from which relations began to improve—and with this the realisation that the Fringe is what makes the Edinburgh Festival unique amongst the European arts festivals.

Reproduced courtesy of Scotsman Publications

The Sceptics in *David Hume on God and Evil* **at the Paperback Bookshop in 1961**

The Traverse Theatre Club 1962 to 1976

The Traverse Theatre is the most enduring legacy of the Edinburgh Festival Fringe. Throughout the year it keeps alive the Fringe's adventurous spirit and when August comes round it functions as a base for the fountain of theatrical activity.

Allen Wright, *The Scotsman* 20 November 1970

In 1960 a group who called themselves The Sceptics presented an unusual piece of entertainment in an unusual place. They performed in costume a dramatised version of David Hume's *First Dialogue Concerning Natural Religion* in the Paperback Bookshop at 22a Charles Street. The building has now gone, demolished at the behest of Edinburgh University to make way for a car park, but its descendant has survived in the shape of the Traverse Theatre in the Grassmarket.

The Paperback Bookshop was owned and run by an American, from New Orleans, Jim Haynes. He had studied at Edinburgh University, having previously been in the United States Air Force. His presentation of Hume's work aroused considerable interest. The small playing area in the shop only held about forty people and it was full each night of the 1960 run. The critics were impressed by the way that an eighteenth-century atmosphere was recreated for the piece and the *Scotsman* critic went so far as to say,

> This is probably the contribution to the Festival which owes more than any other to Edinburgh. It can be strongly recommended to anyone who enjoys a good Scottish argument.

The Sceptics were encouraged to return to the Fringe the next year to do the second part of Hume's dialogue which they called *David Hume on God and Evil*. Over claret the actors examined the theological problems posed by the existence of evil. Afterwards they joined in discussion with their audience over the points raised in the play. This sort of participation carried on into the third Fringe at the Paperback Bookshop in 1962. The group had renamed themselves The Curetes and they performed *Ane Tryall of Heretiks* by Fionn MacColla. The Reformation, and a piece of special pleading for the Roman Catholic standpoint formed the basis of the drama. The actors, among them John Malcolm, the artist and critic R. H. Westwater, Andrew Muir and John Wilson, were richly praised in the newspapers at the time and their efforts were also recorded in verse—in Robert Garioch's poem *And They Were Richt*:

> I went to see 'Ane Tryall of Heretiks'
> by Fionn MacColla, treatit as a play;
> a wyce-like wark, but what I want to say
> is mair taen-up wi halie politics
>
> nor wi the piece itsel; the kinna tricks
> the unco-guid get up til whan they hae
> their wey. Yon late-nicht ploy on Setterday
> was thrang wi Protestants and Catholics,
>
> an eydent audience, wi fowth of bricht
> arguments was hae them kept gaun till Monday.
> It seemed discussion wad last out the nicht,

hadna the poliss, sent by Mrs Grundy
pitten us out at twelve. And they were richt!
Wha daur debait religion on a Sunday?

Despite Mrs Grundy, Jim Haynes believed that an important function of the drama at his shop was actively to involve the audience. By asking them to think about what they had seen he hoped to stimulate audiences into being more demanding and more appreciative. Haynes was also bringing actors and audiences physically closer in his tiny theatre, doing the sort of thing the Oxford Theatre Group had been preaching eight years earlier.

At the opening of the 1963 Fringe Club in South St Andrew Street, Kenneth Ireland spoke about the idea of an all-the-year-round Fringe Centre, a permanent theatre which would promote the style of drama which had come to be associated with the Edinburgh Fringe. He also hoped that such a centre would include an exhibition area and in general be more than simply a small, intimate theatre. One of Ireland's assistant stage managers at Pitlochry, Terry Lane, had been involved with the plays and discussions organised by Jim Haynes at his Paperback Bookshop. He must have listened attentively to his boss's words because it was Lane and Jonn Malcolm, an actor from *Ane Tryall of Heretiks*, who began working to establish the Traverse Theatre Club. With Haynes's support, they looked around for suitable premises. At that time John Malcolm was living in a flat in James Court in the Lawnmarket. The property used to be known as 'Kelly's Paradise' and it seems to have been at one time one of Edinburgh's most famous brothels. Significantly the building was used by Cambridge University students at the 1962 Fringe. They had set up a temporary club, the Sphinx, with late cabaret and meals, and it had apparently been a successful enterprise. The owner of this building, Tom Mitchell, was approached by

Reproduced courtesy of Scotsman Publications

Rehearsal for *Huis Clos* by Jean-Paul Sartre, the first production at the Traverse Theatre Club. The picture shows what the old Traverse was like with its seating on either side of the action. In this case the action was not simulated: the actress on the right, Colette O'Neil, was accidentally stabbed during rehearsal and for a time the hospital described her condition as critical

Malcolm, Lane and Haynes with the idea of turning Kelly's Paradise into a permanent theatre club. Mitchell was enthusiastic and work on the conversion probably began in October 1962. In November a committee of management was formed with Tom Mitchell as club President, Jim Haynes as Chairman and Terry Lane and John Malcolm as joint artistic directors. Although Haynes is now seen as the founder and inspiration of the Traverse, it is curious to note that he does not seem to have been in Scotland from late November 1962 until 26 February 1963. He could not have been actively involved in the practical work of creating the theatre nor could he have attended the first few performances.

The playing space which Terry Lane and John Malcolm created in Kelly's Paradise was very small. It held only sixty people and the stage area was tiny. Because the audience sat in two blocks of seating on either side of the stage, it was called the 'Traverse'—the stage 'traversed' the auditorium.

Terry Lane   November 1962–January 1964

Conversion work on the new theatre must have gone well in the last few weeks of 1962 because the committee felt able to publish their programme of plays for the early part of 1963. The programme carried an explanation of what a traverse stage was:

> The convention of traverse theatre is new to Britain and the essential purpose is similar to that of theatre in the round; in that the audience has closer contact with the play. Traverse Theatre is in fact a stage which traverses the auditorium and divides the audience into two blocks; there is no set to hamper the imagination of the audience and everything which happens on stage is at once lifesize and more colourful as a result of the close proximity of the players.

It also gave advance notice that the theatre would open its doors on 2 January 1963 with a double bill: *Orison* by the Spanish playwright Fernando Arrabal, and *Huis Clos* by Jean-Paul Sartre. The first Traverse company was a small one with Collette O'Neil, Tony Healey, Rosamund Dickson, and Clyde Pollit with Terry Lane taking walk-on parts as well as directing. Their first double bill went down well with Ronald Mavor, the *Scotsman* critic. He understood how sixteen Festival Fringes had not only attuned Edinburgh audiences to intimate theatre but also built an audience for an enterprise like the Traverse:

> The small theatre relieves the actor of the necessity of speaking, gesturing and, in general terms, 'projecting' to a large auditorium and it magnifies the qualities of clarity and intelligence in performer and production while, by a sort of inverse Parkinson's Law, the bigger dramatic effect appears no bigger from landing, like a lion in your lap. Niceties of phrase and phrasing become very important. It is difficult not to think of chamber music.

No manifesto could express one of the major purposes of Fringe theatre better than that. Mavor's review also gives information on how the Traverse was organised. It was more than simply a theatre, it had opted to be a theatre club. On several floors at James Court (the property was formerly two flats) there were dressing rooms, scene dock, wardrobe, box office, coffee bar cum gallery, a restaurant, lounge, a bar and of course the playing area. It was well decorated and comfortable, according to Mavor, and the annual subscription amounted to one guinea.

The committee of management decided to constitute the Traverse as a club for two reasons. First an initial flood of guinea subscriptions would prove a handy method of raising the capital needed for such a venture. Second, the office of the Lord Chamberlain still existed in 1963 as a censoring body for the theatre. All new scripts had to be sent there for approval (or not) except for those to be performed in clubs.

dead letter

BY ROBERT PINGET

Translated by Barbara Bray

directed by CALLUM MILL

◄ Maxine Holden

as

LILI

Scottish Premiere

Dead Letter

BRIEF

SOME OUTSTANDING TRAVERSE
PRODUCTIONS IN 1964 . . .

Michael Elwick and John Sheddon in
THE CARETAKER (Pinter) February

The Premiere

THERE WAS A MAN

by TOM WRIGHT

BRITISH PREMIERE Revival

THE OLD TUNE

By ROBERT PINGET

Adapted by Samuel Beckett

LEONARD MAGUIRE
Gorman
DECLAN MULHOLLAND
Cream

The Old Tune was first performed in Britain at the
Traverse Theatre last year and was acclaimed by the
critics. Old age, loneliness, frustration and impotence are
portrayed with rare pathos, feeling and much wry humour,
though always with sympathy and understanding, in the
dialogue which ensues from the meeting of two old men
on a park bench.

Directed by Michael Geliot

THERE AN INTERVAL OF FIFTEEN MINUTES

Paul Kermack ►

as

MONSIEUR LEVERT

◄ David McKail

as THE BARMAN and
THE POST-OFFICE CLERK

Robert Pinget

*Courtesy of
Traverse Theatre Club*

**Early Traverse programmes
and productions**

In his year as Director and Theatre Manager, Terry Lane really laid the foundations of the Traverse's reputation as an exciting, innovative part of the British theatre scene. The range of plays he directed was enormous. Of the twenty-two plays Lane was responsible for, seven were either British or world premieres. Not only were English playwrights represented, there was also work from Italy, Japan, America, France, Spain, Norway, Ireland and Germany. Alongside Noel Coward's *Private Lives* is *The Days and Nights of Beebee Fenstermaker* by William Snyder, or *Candida* by George Bernard Shaw and *Three Modern No Plays* by Yukio Mishima.

The latter provided an interesting experiment for Edinburgh theatre-goers. The *Three No Plays* stem from a tradition of Japanese drama which began as playlets performed at temples and shrines. It was developed into its present form by the fourteenth century. *No* was suitable for production at the Traverse because it employed few actors and told simple, episodic stories. The first playlet, *The Lady Aoi*, is about a man, whose wife, on her bed of sickness, is tortured by the daylight ghost of his first love. The husband's thoughts about the two women are the basis of the drama. The second playlet, *Hanjo*, is about a geisha driven mad by the loss of her lover. She becomes involved in a relationship with another girl who is terrified that the lover will return. But when he does, the geisha, because of her madness, does not recognise him and the relationship between the two women is preserved. *The Damask Drum*, the final playlet, is not so simple as the other two. It concerns a silent and proud lady who is loved by three young men and an old man, the janitor in a neighbouring building. She agrees to accept the janitor's love if he can beat a sound from a silk drum. Even although he succeeds, the lady decides not to accept the old man's love.

Ronald Mavor commented in *The Scotsman*,

What is intriguing about these stories is that the action, such as it is, does not develop or advance the characters or the plot. It simply reveals the situation which has been there all the time. The plays are like paper flowers. They do not grow; they unfold.

Two weeks before the *No* plays were staged, the Traverse Company had tackled *The Days and Nights of Beebee Fenstermaker* by William Snyder. Set in the twentieth century, the action is spread over ten years and concerns the life of Beebee, who has left home. She sets up in an apartment in the big city, full of ideas and literary ambition. Over the ten years Beebee's enthusiasm wears out and her ambitions fade. Her apartment becomes squalid and she runs out of money. In the last scene a young lad turns up from the country and gives Beebee a glimpse of her youth and perhaps saves her soul.

Critics rejoiced to be offered this variety of work and in the main were able to applaud the quality of the acting and the direction. The sheer versatility of the company was in itself impressive and that was balanced by Terry Lane's ingenuity in fitting so many different sorts of plays into the same tight, little space.

However, towards the end of 1963, it became clear that all was not well at the Traverse, despite the excellent critical response to Lane's work. As both artistic director and theatre manager, he was responsible for the deficit of £3000 which had materialised at the end of his first year. The main reason for this seems to have been poor houses with an average of only thirty people at each performance—and this despite a club membership of 2100. Magnus Magnusson wrote in *The Scotsman*, 'Lip-service is not enough to fill the Traverse'. Too many people admired what the theatre was doing without taking the trouble to go along and see it. A large response in the letter page of *The Scotsman* to Magnusson's article reveals some interesting attitudes. Tom Mitchell, the President of the Traverse, wrote to emphasise that whatever the criticisms there now existed a fully equipped theatre club where none had been before. He seems to have been arguing, obliquely, for subsidy. A lady wrote to complain that the Traverse was a club and that this discouraged potential audiences. Another letter complained that programme notes did not help people to understand what were avant-garde plays. Yet another wrote, with an air of resignation, that Edinburgh people were a bunch of savages and that for the culturally-minded it would be more fun to live in the Kalahari desert. On the whole, though, most interested people gave their support to the theatre. The committee of management, for their part, felt that the blame for the Traverse's precarious position lay squarely at the feet of Terry Lane. In mid-January 1964 a series of meetings of the committee of management took place without Lane's presence. Jim Haynes, the chairman, subsequently informed Lane that the committee had resolved to dismiss him. In statements to the Press, Haynes insisted that the financial problems of the theatre were not the reason for the sacking; he felt that there was a need for a change of artistic director. Terry Lane put it more strongly. He claimed that he had lost his job for reasons of petty, personal dislike, and had had no warning of the committee's intentions. The acrimonious bickering which followed the sacking tended to obscure the value of Lane's pioneering work at the Traverse. Although he directed only one world premiere, Stanley Eveling's *The Balachites*, he introduced the work of several important foreign playwrights to this country. He also succeeded in the business of launching the theatre both artistically and as a club. That is always a difficult business and Lane's achievement ought to be more widely recognised.

Traverse Exhibitions

Richard Demarco was on the committee of management from the beginning. He began to develop the restaurant as a gallery with the encouragement of Jim Haynes whose Paperback Bookshop had generally housed both exhibitions and theatre during the Festival Fringe. The early, informal shows included paintings by Demarco himself, photographs by Alan Daiches and abstract constructions by Peter Clapham. Within the theatre buildings at James Court space was severely limited. So, at the 1964 Festival, the Traverse committee decided to expand into a larger space. They persuaded the Bank of Scotland to lend a number of rooms in George Street, opposite the Assembly Rooms. The Traverse Theatre International Contemporary Art Exhibition showed the work of seven artists whose work was new to Edinburgh. In this way the exhibition side of the Traverse adopted a similar artistic policy to the theatre.

The permanent gallery at James Court opened in October 1964 with an exhibition of paintings by Alastair Michie. The work of William Johnston, Louis le Brocquy, Yago Pericot from Barcelona and Douglas Craft from New York figured in a continuing series of shows up until the middle of 1966.

Jim Haynes   January 1964–7 June 1966

Although he seems to have been out of the country while the Traverse was actually being constructed in late 1962, Jim Haynes's influence on the place was always evident until his resignation in the summer of 1966. It seems likely that he did not actually direct any plays himself but rather that he was closely involved in choosing them. One Traverse programme carried a paragraph encouraging authors to send in scripts to the theatre 'and mark them for the attention of Jim Haynes'. The concept of an artistic director has changed since the mid Sixties. When Haynes styled himself thus, he meant that he had overall artistic control at the Traverse but did not direct plays—in the way that the Director of the Edinburgh Festival directs the artistic policy of the event, but takes no actively creative part.

At all events, under Jim Haynes the Traverse began to expand its activities, for example with the opening of the art gallery. In 1964 a series of 'Talk-outs' on cultural issues took place in the theatre. Club members were invited to air their views on subjects like 'Is the end of architecture the end of architecture?'. Sidney Goodsir-Smith and Robin Philipson led a discussion on 'What's wrong, or right with Scottish Art?'. The need for a Scottish National Theatre, the nature of Scottish poetry and folk-song—the range of the talk-outs was wide and attracted great interest, at least initially. The tradition continues today with the occasional staging of 'Traverse Trials'.

Haynes was concerned to extend the appeal of the Traverse to children and to this end he began to plan a Childrens' Theatre Club early in 1966. A series of readings on the British Renaissance (based on the Elizabethan Renaissance looked at through drama) aimed at the 15–18 age group went ahead. A theatre workshop for kids of all ages was also envisaged although Haynes had not succeeded in finding premises for it. It is not clear from the scanty sources whether or not this project got off the ground but it does illustrate Haynes's interest in relating the Traverse to the community.

Several good directors worked under Haynes between 1964 and 1966, the most frequently employed being Charles Marowitz, Calum Mill and Michael Geliot. Along with Anne Stutfield, Paul Kermack and Gerry Slevin, they were responsible for 38 British or world premieres out of a total of 51 plays done during Jim Haynes's regime. Calum Mill, a Scot with a solid reputation as both a director and an actor, took over immediately after Terry Lane was sacked. Towards the end of 1965 Jim Haynes decided that the Traverse should export its work to London—not so much in an effort to gain prestige, but to raise cash. The maximum possible takings in a week at the theatre during this period was £112 and production costs always far exceeded that sum. So, Haynes became an entrepreneur in partnership with Alexander Racolin. They arranged a seven-week season in the New Arts Theatre in London's West End in order to exploit the 1965 Fringe successes. Tom Wright's *There Was A Man*, Paul Ableman's *Green Julia* and C. P. Taylor's *Happy Days Are Here Again* were scheduled to go on. Despite glowing reviews, the members of the New Arts Theatre stayed away in droves and the venture lost well over £1000. *The Scotsman* summed up the episode:

> But it has, at least, proved one thing—that Edinburgh, despised, provincial Edinburgh, is much more capable of supporting a dynamic, adventurous theatre than much-vaunted London is.

A likely reason for the London failure may be that the city did not have a Fringe to build an audience for experimental or new work. In early 1966 a London Traverse Theatre Company was formed to do plays at the Jeanetta Cochrane Theatre in Holborn. Along with Haynes, the director Michael Geliot was involved. The season lasted from 25 April to 16 July with *Bread and Butter* and *Pink Jesus* both by C. P. Taylor, and *Gaiety of Nations* by Alan Seymour. Charles Marowitz also rewrote *Hamlet* into *The British Premiere of Hamlet*. The exercise seems to have fared better than in 1965 and it was repeated the following year. Although Jim Haynes was adventurous for the Traverse, his ideas were naggingly consistent in the way that they lost money, almost without exception. The debts of the theatre grew from a modest £3000 under Terry Lane to £4595 in 1964, when Haynes predicted solvency for the coming year. In fact things got worse despite some meagre help from the Edinburgh Corporation. The Scottish Arts Council had encouraged the theatre to mount British premieres by adopting a policy of guaranteeing these against loss. Nevertheless by 28 April 1966, the Traverse owed £5454 and had only 1718 members.

Jim Haynes's position had perhaps been weakened in mid 1965 when he ceased to be Chairman of the club and remained as Artistic Director only. He found himself at odds with the committee of management in May and June of 1966, when his contention that he had the right to appoint full-time staff was challenged. Haynes insisted that his employment of Jack Henry Moore should stand. The committee found it impossible to sanction the appointment. Haynes offered his resignation and to his horror it was accepted.

The Press reacted to this with great misgivings. Harold Hobson in the *Sunday Times* wrote:

> I cannot think of any happier preliminary to the 1966 Festival than that Mr Haynes should be asked to reconsider his resignation. It is, I repeat, a matter of international importance in the theatre.

With Jim Haynes's departure the Traverse lost its link with its beginnings at the Paperback Bookshop in Charles Street. There is no doubt that the Traverse would not have happened (and continued) without Haynes and that his charm and aggression were invaluable weapons in its frequent tussles for survival. Nevertheless in the absence of the minutes of early committee meetings and other important sources, it is difficult to trace out Haynes's influence in other than general terms. When he left, Haynes complained that he did so because of 'creeping professionalism' and formal restrictions on his activities as Artistic Director. Perhaps he felt that the theatre was losing its early Fringe origins or forgetting them by becoming more established and organised. How one interprets that is largely a matter of taste.

Gordon McDougall   July 1966–31 March 1968

At the press conference announcing his appointment as the new Artistic Director of the Traverse, Gordon McDougall said, 'We shall continue to do new plays, but because they are worthwhile, and not just for the sake of doing them'. He felt also that the theatre should make greater use of documentary techniques so that shows might have a greater relevance to real life. In this way, he might be able to prise the theatre free from its present middle-class audience. McDougall professed admiration for the work of John Osborne as one of the greatest playwrights of the century. And, finally he asserted that Scottish audiences were the most intelligent in the country. All of these themes recur throughout McDougall's stay at the Traverse.

It was not until after the 1966 Festival that McDougall could really influence the Traverse's output. His first plays were by John Osborne, *Inadmissable Evidence* and *Look Back In Anger* presented in repertory. Demand for tickets was too great for the 60-seat theatre to cope with and McDougall farmed out performances to a hallowed old Fringe venue, the YMCA Theatre in South St Andrew Street. He also hoped to do Traverse productions in the Lyceum but alterations to that theatre prevented the scheme from going forward. By these efforts to move Traverse productions into larger venues, McDougall demonstrated his concern that the small size of the theatre at James Court would always make even successful shows uneconomic.

The Traverse had been broke from the day it opened, but during McDougall's stay, financial problems grew steadily worse. By January 1968 the accumulated deficit was estimated at between £10,000 and £11,000 despite a grant of £7000 from the Scottish Arts Council in 1967. McDougall unfortunately made a mistake which did not help: although houses were generally of a healthy size, one controversial production jeopardised grant aid from both the Arts Council and Edinburgh Corporation. This was a show called *Mass in F* which was staged in early 1968 by the Edinburgh Experimental Group. This mainly student company shocked many people by featuring an actress, naked from the waist up, who related her sexual experiences to the audience. Councillor John Kidd attempted to persuade the Corporation to withdraw its grant of £350 and the theatre was suddenly subjected to a rigorous fire safety inspection. The Scottish Arts Council stated that they would not back plays which did not have a licence from the Lord Chamberlain, whose powers had been recently extended to cover theatre clubs. Because the theatre was in a weak financial position, it was forced to accept these constraints on its artistic freedom and withdraw *Mass in F*.

Early in 1967 McDougall attempted to raise income for the Traverse by engineering the transfer of his premiere production of D. H. Lawrence's *Daughter-In-Law* to a West End theatre. When the deal failed to go through, he commented,

> This would have been the first direct transfer from the Traverse to the West End. Apart from the prestige involved, it would have been profitable. It is the only way we can make the theatre pay.

In March of the same year the Traverse renewed its association with the London Traverse Company which operated in the Jeanetta Cochrane Theatre in Holborn. David Pinner's play *Fanghorn* was premiered in Edinburgh but when it arrived in London it was immediately banned by the Lord Chamberlain. Apparently he objected to the central character, a Lesbian with a penchant for leather gear. Despite the fact that the show caused no problems in Scotland the net result was another lost opportunity to improve the Traverse's finances.

As a result of his efforts to transfer plays to London, Gordon McDougall was criticised by those who felt that the Traverse was selling out to London and London tastes. In reply he pointed out that the theatre had from the beginning been run by Americans or Englishmen, and had only done two Scottish plays. And, remarkably unaware of the Traverse's history, McDougall claimed that no Scottish directors had ever worked there.

Throughout his stay in Edinburgh McDougall seems to have been touchy about criticism. He certainly had his successes, notably *Aberfan* which interwove the stories of the tragedy in South Wales and the Tay Bridge Disaster. He used a cast of Edinburgh children to tell the tale of bureaucratic incompetence, and the only adult on stage was Ros Clarke who played their teacher. Allen Wright, the drama critic of *The Scotsman* gave the show a rave notice. Yet when the same critic was less charitable, McDougall wrote a letter to the paper complaining that Wright had failed to take full account of the experimental nature of the Traverse. It was not in business to produce fully finished, polished pieces of work. Allen Wright refuted this, saying that McDougall must not be upset if some of his experiments failed.

By January 1968 Gordon McDougall had decided to leave the Traverse to go back to working in television. He had done several interesting plays, *Women Beware Women* by Thomas Middleton, Samuel Becket's *Waiting For Godot* and another documentary drama *Would You Look At Them Smashing All The Lovely Windows* by David Wright, a play about the Irish troubles. And he had been deeply concerned with the desperate financial plight of the Traverse. In these days of increased subsidy, it is often forgotten how desperately difficult it was simply to keep the theatre going as it lurched from one crisis to another. Headlines like 'Traverse Faced With Closure' appeared regularly. Several individuals guaranteed the theatre's debts or found themselves paying the wages when the bank refused further credit. Life at the Traverse is still tough but perhaps a bit less desperate.

At all events, Gordon McDougall left the Traverse trailing several unfortunate headlines. His words of 1966 when he praised Scottish audiences were very far from his mind as he likened Edinburgh to a cultural desert. He went on,

> To most people in Edinburgh, the Festival is a bore. To most of them the Traverse is a strip club . . . If the Traverse was in London or in any other big provincial city, it would be appreciated a great deal more than it is.

He added that he thought the reputation of the Traverse outside Edinburgh was greater than that of the Lyceum. In this last only, he probably had a point.

Nevertheless Gordon McDougall was not completely disillusioned. He later founded the Stables Theatre for Granada T.V., and he brought his company to the 1969 Festival.

Max Stafford-Clark March 1968–February 1970

Max Stafford-Clark had been associated with the Traverse as early as 1965 when he played August in the premiere production of Robert Shure's *Gloria*. As Gordon McDougall's assistant he directed several plays in 1967 and 1968, including a series of mini-plays at the 1967 Fringe. Stafford-Clark had also travelled to New York to work with the famous La Mama company who first came to the Fringe in 1966 and then the Festival in 1967 and again in 1976. The original connection with the American troupe was the ubiquitous Jim Haynes, but its influence on the Traverse can be seen more readily through Stafford-Clark.

Although Gordon McDougall claimed at the beginning of his period at the Traverse that he was interested in doing new work, he was probably the most conservative director there has been. His major successes were revivals of one sort or another. Stafford-Clarke re-affirmed that 'our primary job is to show Edinburgh audiences avant-garde theatre' at the outset.

Nevertheless he faced the familiar problems of finance. By 1969 the deficit had risen to £11,000 but the threats of closure seemed to be receding. Allen Wright wrote, in 1968, 'The Traverse is now solidly established—which is about the worst fate that can befall this kind of enterprise.' The theatre was losing support in Edinburgh as the novelty wore off, as its freshness dimmed. Wright went on to complain that the Traverse had been too flippant of late and that perhaps that was one of the reasons for its decline.

Time was ripe for a radical change of circumstances to give new impetus to the theatre. This came along in the shape of new premises. The seating capacity at James Court had always been uneconomically small at only sixty and the other facilities there had been cramped, if full of character and cosy charm. Under the leadership of its Chairman, Nicholas Fairbairn, the committee of management resolved to look for new premises. By mid-1969 they had found suitable buildings at 112 West Bow in the Grassmarket. These were a warehouse and a number of smaller rooms. The area intended for the theatre was much larger than at James Court; it could seat 120. The committee drew up an agreement with Dr Edward Butterworth, the owner of 112 West Bow, to lease the premises for eleven years. The Scottish Arts Council came forward with a grant to equip the building as a theatre and a frantic rush began to have it ready for the 1969 Fringe. On 20 August Nicholas Fairbairn duly escorted Jennie Lee, the then Minister for the Arts, through the debris into the new auditorium to open the new Traverse. During the formalities Fairbairn remarked that the Traverse was the only new theatre to be opened since the Edinburgh Festival began—and that was a result of the existence of the Fringe, not the official Festival.

Meanwhile Max Stafford-Clark had been rebuilding another sort of edifice. Every one of the Traverse plays in 1968, since McDougall's departure, had been either British or world premieres. Several of these were put together using workshop techniques; starting from a basic script actors would add to it with their ideas and interpretations. In *Comings and Goings* by Megan Terry, the audience controlled the action. During a scene a baton was passed around the theatre and when one of the audience held it up the actors froze what they were doing. When the baton started moving again the actors continued what they were doing, or another group came on.

In one of several skirmishes with critics (in this at least he was like his predecessor), Stafford-Clark advanced the view that Fringe theatre was becoming a director's theatre and that there were very few good writers around. Perhaps as a result of this view and his association with La Mama, Stafford-Clark began to run daily workshops for his company. In early 1969 he had managed to establish a permanent company of six performers, whereas before actors had usually been taken on for one or two plays only. Stafford-Clark's policy of hiring a permanent company was aimed at forming an individual style— a Traverse style. And to provide 'a workshop force that would be positive help to all writers, whether playwrights or not, working in Scotland'. The first group-workshop production was *Dracula* in February 1969. It involved a team of seven writers working with the company. Stafford-Clark rightly points out that this approach bore fruit with two of the team co-operating in a new play: Robert Nye and Bill Watson wrote *Sawney Bean* for the 1969 Fringe. Alan Jackson, another member of the *Dracula* team wrote *Deacon Brodie, Baby* which Max Stafford-Clark did after he left the Traverse. Stanley Eveling, Claris Erickson (from the La Mama troupe), David Mowat and John Downie were the others involved in the project and all wrote for the Traverse in Stafford-Clark's time.

In 1968 the Traverse company began to be more outgoing with tours to Boston, Baalbek in the Lebanon and the Mickery Theatre in Amsterdam. They also went to the Open Space in London which had been founded by Charles Marowitz. Jim Haynes was in London at that time and a year previously had started the Arts Lab. The growth of the London Fringe in the late Sixties is directly traceable to Haynes's project. In fact the stimulus provided by the Traverse's survival and success in Edinburgh had encouraged many small theatres to open, using it as a model.

Returning to Stafford-Clark, it was clear by early 1970 that he wanted to leave the Traverse to set up his own workshop company. He explained his reasons to *Scottish Theatre*:

> You find that there's only once or maybe twice during any year when you can get yourself this extra freedom to work. No matter how generous and how liberal the theatre, the theatre is geared to a three-week turnround of productions. In that context, it's very difficult to do the kind of work I want to do.

He set up his company as 'Traverse Workshop Company' in the old Traverse in James Court. Their first productions to be done at the new theatre were *Ultramarine* by David Brett, and *Mother Earth* by David McNiven.

Stafford-Clark's two years at the Traverse brought new ideas and new vigour. Not only did the theatre move into larger and altogether more suitable premises, but it also seemed, through his insistence on experiment, to turn its attention back to more definitely theatrical issues. As an individual, Max Stafford-Clark was not too independent to co-exist with his committee and when he left, both parties emphasised that there had been no question of a disagreement. He simply wanted to do his own thing.

Michael Rudman   February 1970–May 1973

The Traverse Workshop Company was one of many visiting troupes using the Traverse at this time. Others included Portable Theatre, the London Theatre Group, Low Moan Spectacular and the Freehold Company. Traverse-originated productions employed actors for only a few weeks at a time and the year was not divided between a short visiting companies season and a long Traverse company season as it is now. Because of the indiscriminate way in which reviewers write about Traverse shows it is very difficult to sort out the artistic policy of a Director. Any list of productions rarely distinguishes between visiting companies and those directed from the Traverse.

Max Stafford-Clark's successor was Michael Rudman. An American, he had taken a degree at Oxford and directed two productions for the Oxford Theatre Group on the Fringe in the Sixties. He then went to the Nottingham Playhouse for five years where he worked with John Neville, latterly as Associate Director.

At the press conference announcing his appointment Rudman made no large promises, saying that he would settle for the Traverse being 'the best theatre in the Grassmarket'. He observed that Edinburgh audiences were sophisticated and adventurous in their tastes, although predominantly middle-class. New work would, of course, be done—as the most important feature of the Traverse was the promotion of experiment and innovation.

Unlike Jim Haynes, Michael Rudman had good relations with his committee of management and unlike both Gordon McDougall and Max Stafford-Clark, he co-existed well with the Press. He even went so far as to agree with Allen Wright over the question of Arts Council help for new plays written by non-Scots or those living outside Scotland. Rudman argued, convincingly, that Scottish theatres suffered because they could not guarantee a non-Scottish play against loss—as part of Scottish Arts Council policy. This meant that English theatres, like the Hampstead Theatre Club, could offer non-Scottish writers a better deal in any competition with the Traverse. If a non-Scots play were successful, a theatre could live well on the royalties, and Scottish theatres were being denied this opportunity by the Scottish Arts Council. Rudman affirmed that he thought Scottish writers should be favoured but not so rigidly.

At a conference in 1972 the topic was a Scottish National Theatre. Michael Rudman gave his views,

> Rudman was blunt and forceful. Theatre should not be narrowly Scottish, nor should any theatre attempt to be chauvinistically national. Any such institution would become merely a monument to the people who made it.
>
> He argued strongly for a conservative policy in the Arts Council, a continuation and improvement of subsidies to existing theatres, with hopefully, help to establish theatres in Aberdeen and Inverness. Although he shared the pessimism about financial viability by all the professional speakers, he advocated compromise and the art of the possible.

By imagining how difficult it would have been for Jim Haynes to say that the Arts Council ought to be conservative and that compromise was necessary, it is possible to see how far the Traverse had come since 1963, and how much attitudes had changed. Michael Rudman was probably the first orthodox Director at the Traverse in that he admitted that it had become established.

The eternal financial problems of the Traverse receded considerably under Rudman's astute direction. In May 1972 he was able to announce an increase of 10,000 in Traverse audiences since he took over. The accumulated deficit had been reduced from £12,800 to the more manageable level of £7000. 25,000 tickets had been sold in the previous year for £18,100. Rudman was neither complacent nor tempted to blow his gains on any extravagant projects. The Arts Council revenue grant stood at £16,500 plus £2000 for visiting companies and a sum to be negotiated for new plays. The grant from the Corporation had been doubled and the Club membership had risen to 3500.

Like his predecessors, Rudman did new plays by Stanley Eveling and C. P. Taylor.

Next Year in Tel Aviv by Taylor, is set in a country cottage where Michael has brought his mistress. He tries to persuade the owner of the cottage, his wife Helen, to allow him to set it up as a love nest, and as a base for a pottery business. It is a commentary on Jewish society (C. P. Taylor himself being of Glasgow Jewish origins) which tries to concentrate on the realities of Jewishness rather than its romantic aspect. Hence the title is not *Next Year in Jerusalem* but *Next Year in Tel Aviv*.

Caravaggio, Buddy is a farce by Stanley Eveling, done on the 1972 Fringe at the Traverse. It is about a painter who keeps trying to kill himself, only to be revived by little green men from outer space. He also gets phone calls from Jesus, climbs Mount Everest, sells one million paintings to a Greek millionaire, and survives the final holocaust to start a new Eden with his dumb girlfriend and the Abominable Snowman. Buddy was played by Ian Holm and the whole mad comedy was well reviewed and played to full houses.

In his years at the Traverse, Rudman was able to choose good performers and writers—and get a consistently large audience for them. He persuaded the Arts Council and the Edinburgh Corporation to grant the theatre much larger sums than hitherto. And he achieved that without impairing the Traverse's artistic freedom. B. A. Young's review of theatre in 1971 reaffirmed the theatre's status:

> And here a side-glance at Edinburgh's Traverse, arguably the most influential theatre in our island, from which so many of the Theatre Upstairs's successes emanate, and others too, like those at the Open Space . . .

Mike Ockrent   May 1973–November 1975

When Michael Rudman moved to become Director of the Hampstead Theatre Club, his place at the Traverse was taken by Mike Ockrent, a Londoner who studied at Edinburgh University in the mid-Sixties. When he left university he became a trainee director with Joan Knight at Perth. During Rudman's time, Ockrent directed C. P. Taylor's *Next Year in Tel Aviv*, and David Halliwell's *Little Malcolm and his Struggle against the Eunuchs*, both Traverse Company productions.

When he took over, Ockrent outlined a policy of doing more plays from outside Britain. The Traverse in Terry Lane's time had chosen work from many countries and this was a tradition to be revived. Designers, Ockrent believed, had not been allowed to exploit the theatre-space fully. But he emphasised that there would be no departure from the Traverse's role in encouraging new writers.

When the 1973 summer programme was announced plays by European playwrights featured prominently. *Kaspar* by the Austrian, Peter Handke, was the first to be done. It is about a young autistic boy who is guided and taught over a period until he can speak again normally. Conor Cruise O'Brien's *King Herod Explains* followed soon after and C. P. Taylor was pressed into service to adapt Bertolt Brecht's *Drums in the Night* which was done by Foco Novo Productions.

Ockrent obtained the committee's approval to employ the Traverse's first resident designer, Diana Greenwood from the Central School of Arts in London. She did costumes and set for *Kaspar*, setting a high standard of work which has been maintained up until the present. The financial stability which allowed such appointments was mainly a result of Michael Rudman's intelligent management but Mike Ockrent was able to reduce the accumulated deficit to a mere £1500 and in 1973 the Arts Council's grant had risen to £28,000. This also permitted more experimentation. Workshop companies like Paradise Foundry (formerly Portable Theatre) came with their production of Snoo Wilson's *Vampire*, and the Traverse Student Workshop began to mount productions in 1974. Discussions after performances were also revived—these had been a feature of Jim

Haynes's early work at the Paperback Bookshop—in an effort to bring the actors and the members of the theatre club closer together.

More dance and mime was done at the Traverse during this period. The Long Green Theatre Company, Lindsay Kemp Theatre Troupe (both of these based in Edinburgh) and the Will Spoor Troupe all did performances in 1973 and 1974.

Much the best and most widely reviewed production done at the theatre was a double bill of plays by Brecht, *The Measures Taken* and *The Exception and the Rule*. These were directed by a visiting Rumanian, Radu Penciulescu. By contrast, the most controversial play since *Mass in F* was done by an American company, the San Quentin Drama Workshop. The play *Bug*, by Rick Cluchey and R. S. Bailey, was destroyed by the critics for its obscenity, but more important it brought howls of pain from several councillors. Moves were made to have Edinburgh Corporation's grant removed by people who, as usual, had not seen the show. This familiar scenario pointed up the sad fact that the Traverse had begun again to slip into serious debt. Yet, as a result of simply hanging on and surviving, there was never much doubt that the Traverse would survive. It had by the end of Mike Ockrent's tenure been through too many battles to go under in 1975.

Chris Parr   November 1975–

In November of that year Ockrent left to be replaced by the present Director, Chris Parr. Like most of his predecessors, Parr had served his apprenticeship on the Fringe, his most successful production being *The Quest* by Richard Crane for Bradford University Drama Group.

It would be fatuous to try to evaluate Chris Parr's contribution to the Traverse before it is over, but it is possible to point to a strong change of emphasis from Mike Ockrent. Instead of looking outside Britain for plays, he has made it a policy to encourage Scottish playwrights, notably Donald Campbell with *The Jesuit*, about St John Ogilvie—surely one of the most powerful pieces of drama anywhere in 1976—and Hector MacMillan with *The Gay Gorbals*, a truly hilarious farce which revolves around one man's attempt to set up a club for gays in Glasgow. *The Hard Man* by Tom McGrath is about the life of a Glasgow gangster, based on the story of Jimmy Boyle. It has been widely praised, and at the time of writing is touring all over Britain.

Also, Parr has introduced a better-organised distinction between visiting companies who have a short season between the Festival and mid-January, and the resident company who perform for the rest of the year. With a professional Administrator and a committee of very practical people, it seems likely that the Traverse will continue and flourish artistically although it is inescapable that the theatre has had to become part of the 'establishment' in order to do that. The freshness and danger of the early days at James Court have, quite properly, disappeared. But the Traverse's present vitality stems definitely from the early trail-blazing—and sheer faith of people like Jim Haynes. Here is what Ronald Mavor, the *Scotsman* drama critic before Allen Wright, said about Haynes:

> Jim was everybody's easy friend and was always on the verge of getting Orson Welles to play King Lear with music by Lionel Bart or Stravinsky on a cart in James Court. Jim's greatest gift was to believe anything possible and, by gentle enthusiasm, to keep everybody's daft notions alive until, almost as often as not, they began to take shape. Everybody went to the Traverse and Jim would introduce you to Timothy Leary, the Lord Provost, and a man who was growing blue carrots in the interval between the acts.

Performances 1963 to 1965

The remarkable thing about the 1963 Fringe was the Traverse Theatre Club. This was its first Fringe and its first opportunity to come to the notice of the world's theatre press. Three productions were presented: the world premiere of Stanley Eveling's *The Balachites*—the first in a long line of Eveling plays done at the Traverse; the British premiere of Alfred Jarry's *Ubu Roi*; and another British premiere, *Comedy, Satire, Irony and Deeper Meaning* by Christian-Dietrich Grabbe. This was a typically eclectic mixture; a new play by a writer living in Edinburgh, a French play first published in 1896 and a comedy written in 1822 and premiered in the Munich Schauspielhaus in 1907. All these were directed by Terry Lane and they drew favourable critical attention to the Traverse.

The Fringe Programme itself also had a new breadth to it. There were three opera companies: St Andrews University did *Bastien and Bastienne* by Mozart and *The Night Bell* by Donizetti, the Abbey Hey Group (from Edinburgh) did a new opera *Gracious Living*, and the Focus Opera Group did three short pieces including *The Telephone* by Menotti. Ballet was put on at the Central Halls by the Irish Folk Ballet. They did work which had been developed from Irish short stories and legends.

Perhaps the most interesting feature of the 1963 Fringe was its size. There were 39 groups in the Programme in addition to several who were not. This made it, by far, the largest Fringe to date.

It is in the nature of the Fringe to fluctuate, however, and in 1964 only 32 groups arrived in Edinburgh. Nevertheless it expanded geographically. Groups took shows out to the suburbs; the Edinburgh Revue Group did *The British Suburban Revue* in its proper setting, a church hall in Joppa, a district of Portobello. City of Coventry Training College did a triple bill in the Dunedin Hall, a masonic lodge in Morningside Drive on the southern edge of the city. This reflects one of the most important developments of this and later years—that groups took their shows to residential areas, making it easier for people to get over some of the social barriers which prevent all sorts of individuals from enjoying the theatre comfortably.

While groups looked for existing halls to perform in, the Royal College of Art Theatre Group brought their theatre with them. They erected a circus big-top on some open ground near the McEwan Hall. Their show was *The Circus, A Man And A Circus Ring*. Most of it was mimed and it concerned the efforts of a young man who wanted to join the circus, but was rejected by the other performers. Critics were mainly puzzled by the show and Ronald Mavor called it, 'The least likely [Fringe show] since Douglas Young's *Puddocks* in the open air at the Braids six years ago.'

The year 1964 proved a good one for revue with Oxford and Cambridge Footlights on top form. With the latter were Richard Eyre, Eric Idle and Graeme Garden and with Oxford Michael Palin and Terry Jones—a Goodie and and three Pythons illustrating the role of the Fringe in encouraging good comic talents at a crucial early stage.

The Traverse in 1964 spilled over into the Pollock Memorial Hall in Marshall Street (another hall demolished in Edinburgh University's redevelopment of the South Side). The show was *Happy End* by Bertolt Brecht and Kurt Weill and it was directed by Michael Geliot. In true Traverse tradition this was the British premiere and the first time the show had been performed outside Germany. The plot, or libretto, chronicles an encounter between The Salvation Army and a group of gangsters. Lieutenant Lillian Holliday attempts to convert the mobsters but finds herself tangled up in one of their criminal ploys. It all, of course, ends happily. Like *Threepenny Opera* and the *Rise and Fall of the City of Mahagonny*, *Happy End* is a musical play with some memorable songs; *Surabaya Johnny*, *Bilbao Song*, *The Sailor's Song*. The critics heaped praise on the show, especially the performances of Bettina Jonic as Lillian Holliday and David Bauer as Bill Cracker, the two principals. *Happy End* was by far the most successful Traverse offering of the 1964 Fringe, but it was not their only one. J. W. Lambert of the *Sunday Times* catalogues the fare on offer:

> Edinburgh may count itself lucky in possessing its own extremely lively arts organisation, in the shape of the Traverse Theatre Club, which ranges more widely than its name suggests. It is currently mounting an exhibition of international contemporary art: sculpture and constructions in the mode of the moment—comically bizarre and spikily menacing. In its own theatre, poetry readings, and folk song in the small hours, supplement no fewer than four British premieres, including works by Ghelderode, Frisch and Mrozek.

The Prospice Players from Kingston Upon Hull Training College had been coming to the Fringe since 1960 presenting mainly Shakespeare. They were an amateur company directed by T. G. Martin, a lecturer in drama at Hull Training College. Done in a traditional fashion, their productions usually earned considerable praise for evenness and consistency. In 1964 *Othello* was Martin's choice and it seemed to have paid off. Here is W. A. Darlington in *The Daily Telegraph*:

> The Hull 'Othello', David Kemp, a big man with a big bass voice, gave the great speeches much of the music Sir Laurence denied them and gave me a corresponding lift of heart.

Apart from the Traverse and Chris Barber's Jazz Band, the 1965 Fringe seems to have been a wholly amateur affair. It represents the point at which professional participation was at its lowest before it began to build up to its present level of sixty to seventy companies, many of whom are now 'Fringe' in the sense that they can set up quickly, almost anywhere. Because official drama was not thought to be good at that time, John Calder made a plea, speaking at the Fringe Club, for a professional Fringe. He wanted to see an artistic director in charge with the power to commission plays and invite specific groups to perform them. Calder was also anxious to see groups touring Scotland before and after the Festival using their techniques for temporary theatre to set up in any handy space. In all this he was curiously anachronistic. There were no touring groups at the time who could do what he advocated and, as has been stated, only two or three professional elements in the Fringe. Yet, apart from his plea for an artistic director for the Edinburgh Fringe, all of what he said has come to seem like a prophecy.

 # Theatre Workshop Edinburgh

At the Traverse Jim Haynes had attempted to start a children's theatre club with workshops and formal performances. Like so much that came from Haynes's fertile imagination, it was left to someone else to bring it to life. In 1965 Ros Clark and Katherine Robins created Theatre Workshop as an arts and drama centre for children. Its first home was in the Traverse rehearsal rooms in York Place and then at St Mark's Unitarian Church where a sympathetic minister allowed his tiny church hall to be used for workshop sessions. Ros Clark was the only adult in *Aberfan*, a play about the tragedy in South Wales, which had its premiere at the Traverse in James Court. Prior to that several original plays for children were done in various halls around Edinburgh.

By 1970 Theatre Workshop came formally into the Fringe Programme with a play called *Telephone* which they performed at St Giles House. In the same year Reg Bolton was appointed Director and permanent premises were found at 66 Hanover Street (near the building which came to be occupied by the Pool Lunch Hour Theatre). In 1972, Edinburgh Corporation gave Theatre Workshop its first annual revenue grant of £2000. Activities expanded and workshop sessions were held in more than 75 schools, colleges, clubs and community centres. The following year performances were given both at the Traverse and the Pool and over 16,000 children were involved. The Workshop was forced to vacate its premises at Hanover Street and was eventually re-housed, temporarily, at Castle Hill School, next door to Edinburgh Castle. In 1974 permanent premises were found at 34 Hamilton Place in Stockbridge and funds were sought from government bodies and private trusts. Finally in 1977 Theatre Workshop did its Fringe shows in its own theatre, which had been three years in the making.

Performances and Exhibitions 1966

The year 1966 was seminal for the Edinburgh Fringe. The Traverse Theatre Club had elected a largely new committee of management which had accepted the resignation of Jim Haynes who departed to London to sow the seeds of the Fringe there. Richard Demarco also departed from his position as the Traverse's Gallery Director. He travelled only as far as Edinburgh's New Town where he set up his own gallery. The third event which marked out 1966 as an important year was the premiere of Tom Stoppard's *Rosencrantz and Guildenstern Are Dead*.

In London, fringe theatre blossomed. After two years with the London Traverse Company Jim Haynes founded the Arts Lab in Drury Lane in 1968. Like the Traverse, this was a haven for the experimental and avant-garde. Haynes put on the first People Shows there, as well as the Pip Simmons Theatre Group, Wherehouse/La Mama Company, Portable Theatre, and the Freehold Company. All of these companies had been seen at the Edinburgh Fringe but not frequently, or obviously in London.

Also in 1968 Charles Marowitz opened the Open Space in Tottenham Court Road. He had directed plays at the Traverse and had seen how a small theatre club could flourish in Edinburgh. The Open Space was organised in a similar way. Within six weeks of opening it had 4000 members and its first show *Fortune and Mens' Eyes* was a runaway success. It transferred very quickly to the West End, creating instant prestige and welcome revenue for the new theatre.

At the same time a former American businessman, Ed Berman, was setting up his Inter Action group with the help of Jean-Pierre Voos, whose International Theatre Club performed at the 1967 Fringe. Berman's group set up a fringe theatre first of all in Queensway. They called it 'Ambiance'. The theatre later moved to Soho where it became known as 'The Almost Free Theatre'.

These elements formed the basis of the London Fringe which has now blossomed into 57 more or less permanent theatre-spaces. The original connection with the Traverse and the Edinburgh Fringe is unmistakable although it is curious to note that the prime movers were all Americans.

Returning to the Traverse itself, Richard Demarco had been expanding the range of the Gallery's activities. The University of Durham had mounted a major Traverse Gallery exhibition in 1966 and Demarco had sent shows to several other universities. As a

La Mama Experimental Theatre Company, 1967 Fringe. The lady (upside down) on the right is Beth Porter, who recently starred with Julie Covington in *Rock Follies*

member of the committee of management, he tried to persuade his colleagues to allow this side of the theatre's activities to expand. When he found them unwilling, Demarco resolved to set up his own art gallery. With the help of Andrew Elliott, James Walker and John Martin, he found premises at 8 Melville Crescent in Edinburgh's Georgian New Town. The Richard Demarco Gallery was begun in the style of a dealer's gallery showing work for sale to private patrons. There were two floors used as exhibition spaces with a cafe in the basement of the building.

Performances at the gallery began with a recital by the tenor, Kevin Miller, in March 1967. Lectures went on frequently, but Demarco really acquired a reputation as an imaginative theatrical entrepreneur with a show by Clive James, now *The Observer*'s TV critic, and Tony Buffery in 1968. And in association with Jim Haynes's Arts Lab, he mounted a show by Geoff Moore's modern dance company, Moving Being, at the 1969 Fringe. The dancers were accompanied by the Incredible String Band. Lindsay Kemp and Nancy Cole both did shows at Melville Crescent in late 1969. But it was with eastern European groups that Demarco made an innovative contribution to the performing arts on the Edinburgh Fringe. From Rumania he brought Miriam Raducanu's dance group in 1971 and the following year Tadeusz Kantor's Cricot Theatre 2. They did a memorable production, *The Water Hen* in a hall known as 'the Poorhouse' in Forrest Hill. Kantor came to the Fringe again in 1973 with *Lovelies and Dowdies*, and again in 1976 with *The Dead Class*. This last was a devastating piece of theatre literally conducted by Kantor himself on stage. It begins with the audience being kept waiting in the foyer until everyone has arrived. Then the doors fly open and people are hustled quickly into seats to the accompaniment of crashingly loud waltz music. Lines of life size dummies sit in rows of school desks on stage confronting the audience. The action of the play is concerned with ageing and death. Although parts of it were hard to understand, *The Dead Class* left some powerful images in the mind. (See photograph on page 118.)

Richard Demarco has his critics and many complain that his gallery receives far too much subsidy from the Scottish Arts Council, but it must be said in his defence that, out of the Traverse, he has made some solid contributions to the Edinburgh Fringe both with performing groups and visual art exhibitions.

Somewhat less solid is the myth that in the same year as Demarco founded his gallery, the Fringe 'discovered' Tom Stoppard and his play *Rosencrantz and Guildenstern Are Dead*. This was premiered by the Oxford Theatre Group at the Cranston Street Hall on 24 August 1966. It began life as a one-act play and was performed by the Questor's Company in 1964 in Ealing. Stoppard rewrote the play into two acts and on the strength of these the Royal Shakespeare Company commissioned a third act. For some reason they never performed it, and after having been read by many people the play came into the hands of the Oxford Theatre Group.

Stoppard himself had written a novel and several radio plays and his first play *A Walk on the Water* was staged in 1960 in Hamburg and Vienna. An adaptation was planned for the London stage in late 1966. So, it was no unknown who had written a completely pristine work for the Oxford Theatre Group. The first night audience at Cranston Street Hall was not large—it apparently consisted of six critics and one lone civilian. Allen Wright of *The Scotsman* felt that the play was 'no more than a clever revue sketch which has got out of hand' and that it was rather badly acted to boot. Harold Hobson of *The Sunday Times* thought that, 'the result is perhaps merely a literary and theatrical curiosity, offering neither guarantee nor bar to Mr Stoppard's future as a dramatist'. John Kerr of *The Glasgow Herald* was even less enthusiastic: 'Mr Stoppard has succeeded only, however, in perpetrating a caprice that contributes little to the medium in which he has chosen to express it.' It was Ronald Bryden's review in *The Observer* which 'made' the play:

The best thing so far at Edinburgh is the new play by Tom Stoppard. He has taken up the vestigial lives of Hamlet's two Wittenberg cronies and made out of them an existentialist fable unabashedly indebted to *Waiting For Godot* but as witty and vaulting as Beckett's original is despairing.

The play does not pretend to know more of the pair's lives than Shakespeare: its point is, neither do they. While the violent drama at Elsinore unrolls off-stage, occasionally sucking them into its fury, they spin coins endlessly in ante-rooms, wondering what is going on, what will happen next, what will become of them? They sense that they should escape, but what to? The tragedy of Denmark offers them the only significance, the only identity life has held out to them—it offers them roles.

Behind the fantastic comedy, you feel allegoric purposes move: is this our relation to our century, to the idea of death, to war? But while the tragedy unfurls in this comic looking-glass, you're too busy with its stream of ironic invention, metaphysical jokes and linguistic acrobatics to pursue them. Like *Love's Labour's Lost* this is erudite comedy, punning, far-fetched, leaping from depth to dizziness. It's the most brilliant debut by a young playwright since John Arden.

Unlike the other critics Bryden had read the script, and had had a hand in placing it with the Oxford Theatre Group. It is obvious from the review that it was the writer that interested him; he makes no mention of any of the actors or the staging.

But this is not to detract from Stoppard's achievement or Bryden's ability to recognise a good thing when he saw it. The point is that the Fringe did not 'discover' Stoppard or his play. None of the other critics liked it, so that the glare of publicity that the Fringe brings to new plays cannot be said to have helped. It was rather the fact that the Oxford Theatre Group had the intelligence to use the play and the Fringe provided them with a ready opportunity to put it on when professional companies had turned it down.

After its success in Edinburgh *Rosencrantz and Guildenstern Are Dead* transferred very quickly to the National Theatre and thence to Broadway. Both Stoppard and the Oxford Theatre Group made a large amount of money from it, and the royalties have enabled the Oxford group to mount the work of many new writers at the Edinburgh Fringe.

 # American Fringe

In the Sixties a tradition of American groups on the Fringe, both professional and student began to grow. The first group to arrive had what must be the longest name in Fringe history. They were the University of Southern California School of Performing Arts, Drama Department Festival Theatre. They came in 1966 under the direction of Professor John Edward Blankenchip to perform at the Pollock Hall in Marshall Street. Besides plays by Albee, Williams and Wilder, they did works by lesser-known American writers: *John Brown's Body* by Stephen Vincent Benet, *Rashomon* by Fay and Michael Kanin, and *Le Boeuf sur le Toit*, an opera by Jean Cocteau and Darius Milhaud. U.S.C. came to Edinburgh regularly in the Sixties moving from hall to hall before settling on the Brunton Halls at Musselburgh.

In 1967 the La Mama Experimental Theatre Club from New York presented four plays in repertoire at the Barrie Halls in Marshall Street. They did this under the Traverse banner, forming part of their Fringe programme. With much the same ideals as their hosts, La Mama had been performing around fifty plays a year for six years in a small theatre club in New York's East Village. During that time they have pioneered the work of Jean-Claude van Itallie (*America Hurrah*) and Paul Foster (*Tom Paine*). And they had toured Europe extensively before coming to the Fringe.

The Demise of Farmer *Futz* **at the 1967 Fringe: performed by La Mama**

La Mama is Ellen Stewart, the lady whose enthusiasm and energy was the spark from which the company started in 1961. She and Tom O'Horgan ran La Mama and put together the group of actors who toured Europe in the summer months.

One of the four plays they did, *Futz* by Rochelle Owens, caused a great amount of controversy when it was staged during the 1967 Fringe. This example of press sensationalisation of the Fringe was fairly typical (and still is) as a response to the more avant-garde sort of work being done on the Fringe. *Futz* was about bestiality. Farmer Futz carried on an idyllic love affair with a pig. His tastes seriously disturbed the small community he lived in. So much so that his neighbours were forced to lynch Futz.

Ronald Bryden of *The Observer* thought the play to be excellent and wrote an enthusiastic review, *The Scotsman* was also encouraging, seeing *Futz* as a satire on the effects of pornography as well as being very entertaining. The *Scottish Daily Express*, however, saw it all in a different light. 'Filth on the Fringe' raged the headline and Brian Meek, the reporter, demanded that the play be banned immediately—despite the fact that it had a licence from the Lord Chamberlain, and despite the fact that he had not seen it—'It was described to me by a *Scottish Daily Express* critic as "The most shocking play I have ever seen".' Meek goes on to outline the show, at second hand:

> A girl is handled intimately by two men at once . . . a man is suggesting intercourse with a sow . . . another actress bares her bosom before her mentally defective son who had just murdered a girl.

At the end of his article, Brian Meek did make clear to his readers that, 'this play has nothing whatever to do with the official Festival. It is not the responsibility of Mr Peter Diamand, the Festival Director'. The story ran for several days afterwards with various councillors registering their views. Bailie Mrs Mary Robertson-Murray protested: 'Asked if she had seen *Futz*, Mrs Robertson-Murray said: "No, and if it portrays bestiality then I wouldn't waste my time."' Tom O'Horgan, speaking for La Mama, was taken by surprise at the storm which his play had created. But he had the wit to reply to Meek's article: 'We must move the audience—otherwise it might as well be just something to sell toothpaste. We intend to produce a very physical theatre by pushing the limits of physicality to the ultimate.'

The point of quoting this particular episode in its entirety is to show how little this sort of sensationalisation changes over the years, and to show how unimportant the offending play usually is. None of the objectors had seen the show and therefore their objections said more about them (or the paucity of news in Edinburgh in August) than anything else. The same treatment has been meted out to Fringe groups via the pages of other newspapers. The groups are often allowed no form of reply—at least the *Express* afforded La Mama that privilege—and the mud sticks. Reports like Brian Meek's have done a good deal to implant the 'filthy Fringe' notion into the conventional wisdom. This makes life difficult in Edinburgh for the groups and the Fringe Society in its efforts to take theatre to people in Edinburgh. For example, church halls are extensively used, through the goodwill of many congregations, and each time a 'filthy Fringe' story hits the headlines, that good-will can be damaged. No one objects to informed criticism and if that hurts, then that is too bad. But nothing hurts more than the uninformed airing of a string of unbecoming prejudices.

Returning to the Americans on the Fringe, University of Southern California must have inspired others to follow in their footsteps. The Canadian Arts Lab came in 1968 to the Viewforth Centre, an arts centre run by a local church. They performed *Slogans*, an improvised play on the wide theme of what their generation thought and how it behaved. A year later New York City Theater Workshop arrived in Edinburgh. This was a troupe of young actors who had been trained at the workshop. They performed two plays at the

Jordanburn Lecture Theatre in the Royal Edinburgh Hospital. Both were British premieres: *The Flight of the Lindberghs* and *A Lesson in Consent*, written by Bertolt Brecht in collaboration with Kurt Weill and Paul Hindemith.

Nancy Cole first came to the Fringe with her *Gertrude Stein's Gertrude Stein* in 1969. This was a solo performance based on the writings of Miss Stein. It covers her literary creations, her real friends and Paris in the early twentieth century. It is a tour de force by Nancy Cole and she has taken the show all over Europe and to America. As an actress Miss Cole was associated with the La Mama troupe in Paris and was aware of their European 'Fringe' connections. With this experience, she has been able to acquire a great store of information about the Fringe Festivals and small theatres and theatre companies in Europe. Moving around Europe she has passed on the simplest bits of information (like the address of the Edinburgh Fringe Society) to other performers. In this way, through people like Nancy Cole, the Fringe in Edinburgh has become more international, in a thoroughly informal way. And British groups have found themselves touring Europe as a result of contacts made in Edinburgh.

 # Performances 1967 to 1969

As the Sixties went on the quality of performance improved steadily. No doubt the advent of increasing numbers of professional companies helped to achieve this but it is also noticeable that the standard of student work went up. In particular Cambridge University Theatre Company, who were regular attenders at this time, set a high standard. Their *Love's Labour's Lost* in 1967 was something of a triumph, with critical acclaim even reaching down to the bit-players. One actress, Julie Covington, was welcomed in a small part in the Shakespeare play and her singing in the Footlights revue was favourably noticed. The following year Cambridge brought the Brecht-Weill opera *The Rise and Fall of the City of Mahagonny*. Harold Hobson reviewed it with more than mere enthusiasm:

> The whole company is good and Julie Covington who plays Jenny, the prostitute, is shattering. She is quiet and gentle even wistful, in a short lyric scene; for the rest she is devastating in the girl's irresistable, attacking sexuality and formidable powers of defence: she is an erotic machine-gun that shoots dead straight—and if my wife were not looking at me so sternly I would also write of her improvisation during the interval.

To further encourage her, Julie Covington won the Elspeth Douglas Reid Trophy for her performance in *Mahagonny*. This sort of success for an individual performer is a good example of how the Fringe, as an open arena, can throw up amateur talent of the best sort.

On the professional side, the late Sixties saw Fringe companies like Abercorn Productions and Basilica Productions who were specially formed to appear at the Fringe. Abercorn did a mini-festival in 1968 at the YMCA. The premiere of *Chekhov* by Allan Cook traced the playwright's life from 1890 to his death: the name part was taken by John Rhys Thomas. Joy Sinden presented her mime show *Enough Said*, there was a showing of the Carol White film *Cathy Come Home* and an exhibition of John Cohen's work *Creative Colour Photography*. By contrast Basilica put all their efforts into one production. This was *The First Night of Pygmalion* by Richard Huggett. Already well reviewed in London, the play concerned the casting for Shaw's masterpiece, the conflicting personalities of Mrs Patrick Campbell, Beerbohm Tree and Shaw himself. Both of these companies resuscitated a tradition of specially-formed companies that had died out in the late Fifties and early Sixties.

Julie Covington with the Elspeth Douglas Reid award, 1968

The permanent touring companies also made their presence felt. Aside from those sponsored by the Traverse, there was a combine of groups based on premises in Victoria Terrace and in a marquee in the Meadows, Edinburgh's Hyde Park. The Wherehouse La Mama Company, the Will Spoor Mime Theatre, Freehold Company, the People Show and Lindsay Kemp all performed there, but without much success. They had committed the (by now) cardinal sin of not being in the Fringe Programme. The result was that their shows were reviewed late in the Festival and audiences were not large. Nevertheless it was true to say that by 1969, the Edinburgh Fringe had become a regular event for the few touring companies in existence at that time.

The Traverse Theatre's Directors were very aware that the Fringe was their annual opportunity to catch international attention from both critics and visitors. The scope of the theatre's activities was expanding during this period and it reached its greatest flowering in 1967 when the Traverse presented 21 premiere productions of plays, all to be performed in the three-week period of the Festival at the theatre in James Court and the Barrie Halls in Marshall Street. Eleven of their shows were 'mini-plays' directed by Max Stafford-Clark. These were short pieces with a cast of only one or two, and in one case, three. The writers involved were James Saunders, Stanley Eveling, Stewart Conn, Rene de Obaldia, Olwen Wymark, Paul Foster, Patsy Southgate and Michael Jones. Of the more substantial plays at the Traverse, Paul Foster's *The Hessian Corporal* was presented in a double bill with Aeschylus's *The Persians*. The former was about the American War of Independence and the colonists' attack on the barracks of the Hessians, mercenaries hired to the British by the Duke of Hesse. These were thought to be some of Europe's crack troops and it was a signal victory for the Americans when they routed them on Christmas night 1776. The comparison with *The Persians* and the story of the Greek struggle for independence against the might of the Persian Empire is a simple one. Apparently Gordon McDougall exploited both the similarity and the contrast between the two plays in two well-acted productions. He had a strong female element in both casts with Hildegard Neil, Miriam Margolyes and Rosemary McHale.

Sanctity by Robert Head was presented by the International Theatre Club at the Traverse during the 1967 Fringe. This group was the resident professional company at the Mercury Theatre in London. Administered by a charitable trust, their main aim was to be a showcase for new drama from around the world which could be presented in the English language. The Club's Director was Jean-Pierre Voos, who helped Ed Berman set up Inter-Action in 1968 and who now runs Kiss-Oresteia, an international touring company. They performed at the 1976 Fringe, doing Greek drama in English, Latin and Greek.

At all events, their production of *Sanctity* marked out the International Theatre Club as one of the highlights of the 1967 Fringe. It was basically an American play, set in the New York State Penitentiary. The storyline concerns the code of the criminal underworld. Maraschino betrayed Blackout and they both finish up in the same cell in the same gaol. Maraschino is killed ultimately, but not before the play has explored the psychology of the criminal environment.

Elsewhere on the Fringe groups were looking to expand their activities. One surprising source of innovation was the French Institute in Randolph Crescent. The Director had started 'French Fringe' in 1968 'to make up for the continued and disturbing absence of French drama from the Edinburgh Festival'. In 1969 he began to set this to rights in a big way with a huge programme of French music and drama. Eole Theatre from Geneva appeared in 1968 and 1969 with *Le Roi se Meurt* and a double bill of *L'Effet Glapion* by Audiberti and *La Truite de Schubert* by da Costa, respectively. Aquarium Theatre from Paris revived *La Mere Coquette* by Quinault and Jeune Theatre de l'Universite Libre de Bruxelles presented *La Politique des Restes* by Adamov, a piece of agitprop. And Tex, a troupe from Aix en Provence did a revised version of Merimée's *Carmen*. Since then, the French Institute has played an imaginative part both as host and entrepreneur on the Fringe.

In the late Sixties, established groups tended to do a larger programme. Using the revenue from *Rosencrantz and Guildenstern Are Dead* the Oxford Theatre Group did two new plays, the revue and an art exhibition in 1967. Edinburgh University Theatre Company were doing four plays in their fully equipped theatres at Adam House and George Square and, incidentally, were arrogating to themselves—quite erroneously—the title 'Founders of the Fringe'.

In addition the Fringe itself was beginning to expand, very definitely, into the other performing, and visual, arts. Richard Demarco had begun to mount half a dozen exhibitions at his gallery in Melville Crescent and local artists were coming into the Fringe Programme with small exhibitions of their work. There had always been a large fringe-of-the-Fringe since the earliest Festivals and it had consisted mainly of exhibitions. It was not the case that (Demarco apart) the Fringe was stimulating more activity in the visual arts, but rather that its Programme was providing a showcase where artists' work could be noticed.

Music, as distinct from musicals or plays with music, was also coming increasingly to the fore. The Reid School of Music at Edinburgh had begun to let its concert hall to Fringe groups and in 1968 the London Chamber Opera performed there. They did two short pieces: *Agar et Ismaele Esiliati* which was a staged version of Alessandro Scarlatti's oratorio of 1683, and *La Zingara* a comic intermezzo by Rinaldo da Capua. A chamber music ensemble called Musica Antica e Nuova performed in the National Library of Scotland during this period. They concentrated on the work of little-known composers like Joh, Couperin, Clementi and Sciabine, and that of moderns like Thea Musgrave. As more of these small professional music groups began to come, the Fringe acquired a reputation for complementing the Festival's interest in large scale popular works with small scale, unusual pieces for those with an informed interest in music—and those whose finances would not stretch to take in the entire Festival music programme.

Because of its internationalist nature—messages without words—mime became popular and troupes or soloists from abroad have gradually become a part of the Fringe. In 1969 Adam Darius, a leading American mime performed in a hall in Shandwick Place and from Greece, Photis Constantinidis did a show which tried to express man's attempts at survival after a holocaust has destroyed society. His work was very well received.

> Standing alone on a bare stage, Photis Constantinidis mimes—and rivets the attention of an enthralled audience. His extraordinarily expressive face, body and hands create an image that is clear and unambiguous, and as often deeply moving as irreverently witty.

British companies of dancers were also becoming popular. At the Demarco Gallery there were performances from Moving Being, a small professional group. At Portobello Town Hall there was Ballet Lurdan, a privately backed company whose aim was to present young professional dancers in original works by young choreographers. A former member of Joan Littlewood's Theatre Workshop, Hettie Loman, formed a similar company which was oriented towards a contemporary European style. A Scottish American Ballet company was formed for the 1969 Fringe using dancers from the Alabama State Ballet and Marjory Middleton's Edinburgh Ballet Theatre. They too performed some new pieces including the third act of a new version of Prokofiev's *Romeo and Juliet* which had recently been premiered in the United States.

Mostly professionals, these groups provided a strong element in the Fringe and one which, every year attracts a growing audience for dance and mime.

Moving Being in *Sun* **directed and choreographed by Geoff Moore at the 1972 Fringe**

The Fringe Programme has always contained surprises; the Scottish Horse Show, the odd Highland Games, advertisements for Zen Buddhism and suchlike, and it has often covered performances which do not strictly come into drama, music, mime, dance or revue. The Purves Puppets are based in West Lothian. They began in the Fringe in 1963 and have appeared ever since at St George's West Church Hall in Shandwick Place. They have become a completely professional outfit doing childrens' shows all over Scotland, starting their summer season in July and ending after the Fringe. Films have occasionally been shown in Fringe halls, and in 1967 a literary dimension sprang up in the shape of *The Alchemist*. This was a magazine published in Edinburgh by students from the Oxford Theatre Group. It included contributions from Harold Hobson, Kingsley Amis and, interestingly, Mary Whitehouse. Nowadays small groups of writers and poets sometimes produce a 'special' for the Fringe audiences to read in their few spare moments.

At all events, the late Sixties saw an efflorescence of all the arts. The Fringe began to encompass almost every conceivable form of visual arts and performance which the Festival did not present, or coped with in a different way. The entire Festival event, including the Fringe, the official Festival, and the Film Festival, could be seen at the end of the Sixties as a comprehensive review of the arts in Western Europe.

 # The Festival Fringe Society Limited

By 1969 the Fringe had grown to 57 groups doing more than 100 shows. As this expansion put strain on the volunteers who ran the Fringe Society, it became clear that professional advice as to the future structure of the Society might be useful. The committee co-opted Andrew Kerr, an Edinburgh solicitor, who recommended that the Society should be incorporated as a company limited by guarantee, with charitable status. Groups would be eligible for membership and there would be a Board of Directors in addition to, and eventually in place of, the committee. Kerr suggested that the relative formality of such a structure would make the Society (as it would continue to be called) a more attractive subject for grants and donations, and that it would offer a simple means of allowing groups an appropriate say in the Society's organisation. He was authorised to proceed at the end of 1967, but adjusting the draft Memorandum and Articles with the Inland Revenue to ensure that charitable status would be achieved took much longer than had been expected, and the new company was not incorporated, as 'Festival Fringe Society Limited', until 22 May 1969. Andrew Kerr became Company Secretary (or, strictly, his firm—Bell & Scott, Bruce & Kerr, W. S.—became Company Secretaries), and George Shaw, a bank manager, became Treasurer, handing over to Leslie Bennie, who had been Vice-Chairman of the Traverse, in 1972. There were seven Directors initially (there are now fourteen, and there were until recently fifteen, the maximum allowed by the Articles). The first Chairman was Lord Grant, Lord Justice-Clerk and Vice-Chairman of the Directors of Scottish Opera, and the committee was dissolved in November 1971.

Continuous expansion made it increasingly difficult for an entirely voluntary body to offer an acceptable service, and at the 1970 Annual General Meeting the groups more or less demanded that a professional administrator should be appointed. An approach to the Scottish Arts Council in March 1970 for a revenue grant had been a failure, but despite this the Board decided to commit all the available funds to such an appointment. The binding thread running through the next part of the book is the effect of this professionalism on the Fringe.

PART FOUR

1970
TO
1977

John Milligan, Administrator
1971 to 1975

With £700 at their disposal the Board of Directors could only afford to advertise for a part-time administrator. They interviewed a surprisingly large number of candidates and appointed John Milligan in December of 1970.

Milligan was a teacher of art who had worked for the Scottish Arts Council and had been a researcher for the BBC series *Scope*. Initially he worked a three-day week when his appointment commenced in January 1971. His offices were in a room in James Court opposite the old Traverse Theatre. By the time he left the Fringe in 1975, John Milligan had converted his job into more than a full-time occupation; he had created a definitive form for the massive Fringe programme, had found a permanent home for the Fringe Club and had anchored the administration of the Fringe on a sound footing. The effects of his work will be observable all through this part of the book.

Milligan's views on the Fringe itself, as a phenomenon, are on record in a lengthy article which appeared in a 1975 edition of *Festival Times* (a newspaper brought out each Festival by Edinburgh University Student Publications Board see page 125). On a broad level it summed up, for Milligan, the essentially democratic nature of the Fringe, both for performers and audiences:

> So, we have this unique event where anybody can realise their plans of making their own choice on their initiative at their own risk, and it has gathered about it an audience which has own ways of reckoning risk and exercising choice. The audience votes with its seats, sometimes chancing upon a gem, sometimes suffering a lulu. And this is where *Festival Times* along with the rest of the Press comes in. Theirs is an old and honourable craft—to record the transport of a moment seen or felt for the real guidance of readers now and way into the future.

And his views on the Fringe administration:

> The artists come first and the Fringe Society has lit upon a model co-operative in an area endemic with individualism, falling-out, collapsed brotherhoods and movements. It has succeeded because it looks after the public and the artists look after themselves. This laissez-faire has not produced a lazy fair, quite the reverse, and it is clearly more Art and more successful than many's a festival of (dare I say it) recreation and leisure which lacks the magic ingredient—people.

What emerges from his period as administrator is that Milligan believed implicitly in the democracy not only of Fringe but of the arts in general. In 1971 there was a historical need for just such a set of principles for the Fringe. The Society had come to be made up of so many different and potentially divergent parts that there was a real danger of a split. A fringe-of-the-Fringe, or several fringes (aside from the large numbers of exhibitions already existing outside the Fringe programme) could easily have sprung up. Milligan's role was first to show complete impartiality in his treatment of the groups and all-round efficiency in his presentation of them to the public. The above extracts give an idea of how the logic of the historical situation resolved itself, in Milligan's mind, into a system for thinking about the Arts.

As the number of groups taking part in the Fringe grew each year newspapers expressed the view that 'the Fringe has reached its peak'. In 1970 there were nearly 60 companies and the following year 78. The size of the Fringe has only once declined since a professional administrator has run it. There are two reasons for this: first the efficiency of the central administration encouraged more and more groups to take the considerable risk of doing their own thing, and second, the openness of the Fringe itself has attracted those who would otherwise have had no opportunity to present their work to the public and the leading critics. The latter reason is a function of the gradual shrinkage of public funds available to the arts and is the main reason why a flourishing Fringe can seem such an anomaly in an otherwise bleak arts scene.

Halls had always been a problem to groups coming to Edinburgh: there never seemed to be enough of them. In 1969 the congestion was eased when Edinburgh Corporation allowed the Fringe to use school halls for the first time. Nowadays around twenty groups use fifteen or so halls, thereby involving the community more and adding revenue to the local government purse. In 1971 John Milligan was able to incorporate more groups by suggesting that halls should be shared more often. This cut costs and helped groups to stay in the centre of the city.

 # Performances 1970 to 1971

As numbers rose so the quality of work seemed to improve. 1970 was a good year. At the Heriot Watt University Students' Union in Grindlay Street (opposite the Royal Lyceum) a group of performers established 'Fort Knox'. They also called it the New Edinburgh Arts Complex. The programme included plays by Sartre, Alan Ayckbourn and Andy Davis, poetry readings with MacDiarmid, Garioch, McCaig, Morgan and Jackson, revues, an exhibition of constructions by James Goodall, folk music and jazz, a fashion show and a cafe. The whole mini-festival finished with the Fort Knox Golden Ball.

A Game Called Arthur by David Snodin was the Oxford Theatre Group's offering at the 1970 Fringe. It was later transferred to the Traverse for a professional production where it improved as a result. Here is *The Scotsman*'s guarded verdict:

> The play is acted with poise and style throughout, though it comes over much better in the lighter first act than in the second, where the three characters sit through a long, drunken, and at times too melodramatic, night trying to probe deeper mysteries. Playing the main part is the young actor who has taken refuge from his social inadequacy in homosexuality, the author is convincing, intense and febrile, though perhaps overdoing his display of the tricks of the trade— the sweeping gestures, the variation of pitch and speed, the changes of volume and vocal texture.

Like Fort Knox, there was another mini-festival in the 1970 Fringe. This was a combine of several London Fringe groups at the Cranston Street Hall. Theatre Nucleus did *The Poet And The Women* by Aristophanes, the Soho Theatre presented *The Solemn Communion* by Fernando Arrabal. Evidently *The Guardian* described this last as 'amazing and extraordinary', *The Scottish Daily Express* called it 'filth'. The Low Moan Spectacular and Robin Culver also shared Cranston Street Hall, but the group who attracted most attention was the Pip Simmons Theatre Group, one of the oldest Fringe touring companies:

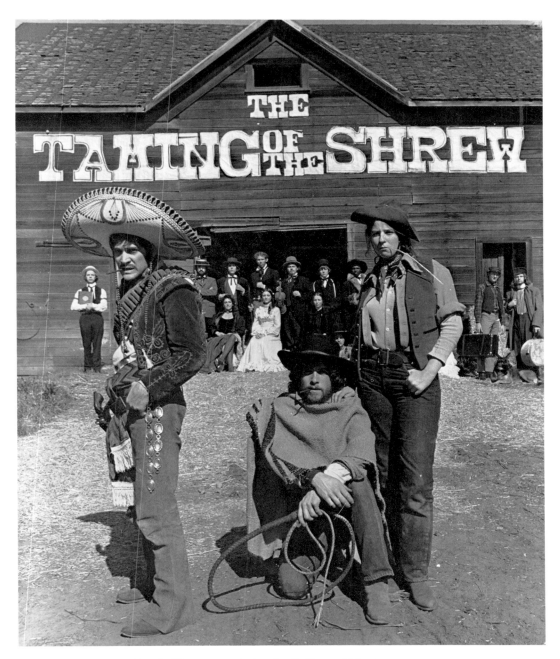

The Taming of the Shrew **in Western style by the College of Maria, 1971**

In a 'rock and roll comic-strip' with Superman in a massive papier-mâche head, the London-based Pip Simmons Theatre Group present four men and two girls, playing their own music, singing, shouting, dancing. They wear padded American football jerseys—one is in blackface, another has an Indian head-dress. They are new to the Festival—and brilliant.

Comic-strip style is visual, exaggerated and rowdy. Mixing it with a basically rock/jazz score by Chris Jordan, this thoroughly professional group weave an extraordinary pattern of sounds and movements whose expressiveness is hard to describe in words.

Inhabiting the bizarre city of Metropolis, the play explored the turmoil, lunacy and fantasy of modern American life in brief, stabbing sketches. But beyond that, Superman is both the kingly Everyman all citizens dream of, and a tormented, vengeful hero. He reaches back to the endless myths of the pained human mind.

Such total theatre can be atrocious when it is in the least sloppy. But these actors use every resource they can find within their own bodies and imaginations, with complete discipline. Definitely worth finding time for.

The Fringe had long enjoyed a tradition of good one-man shows. Calum Mill's portrayal of the 19th-century Edinburgh actor, Charles Mackay, in Donald Mackenzie's *The Bailie* was another premiere production which rated rave notices and it was revived on the 1977 Fringe by Colin Brown.

The American element in the Fringe Programme had been growing steadily since 1966, and two more groups arrived to perform in Edinburgh in 1971. The University of Rhode Island presented *The Beard* by Michael McClure at the Heriot Watt Union in Grindlay Street. The play is about two characters, Billy the Kid and Jean Harlow, and how they set about courtship. The more they rage at each other the better they understand what is happening. Both audiences and critics enjoyed it hugely and, under the highly capable direction of Kimber Wheelock, the Rhode Island troupe have returned with fresh work almost every year since.

The second American group, the College of Marin from California, did a Wild-West version of *The Taming of the Shrew* which seems to have sold out every night of its run, and gathered rapturous reviews. Both of these groups brought tastes of a different but related culture to Edinburgh and theirs was a large gamble which came off—and their enterprise can be seen as a happy advertisement for the openness of the Fringe. Too often new ideas with a good deal of merit get buried in the rush to grab audiences and reviews.

'Sex is alive and in decent health this year on the Edinburgh Festival Fringe' pronounced *The Guardian* in 1971, and it does seem to have been true. Occasionally Fringes do have a theme, or rather a tone which helps to identify them, one from another, although its size does make any total description more than a little shaky. Nevertheless, in 1971 nudity, buggery, fetishism, voyeurism and even heterosexuality seem to have been very much in evidence. Tom Mallin's *The Novelist* was done at the Traverse, starring Barbara Jefford, John Turner and Robin Bailey. It is about a novelist who refuses, despite his wife's entreaties, to see an old friend who has come to visit him. When the friend is finally ushered in, the novelist tries to get rid of him by making a homosexual advance. To add to the complications his wife claims that the friend had her on the kitchen table while he was waiting. The play ends with the friend returning to say that he really found the novelist's advances sympathetic. In fact, the play had much more to say than the plot indicates but it turned on sexual relationships to work out its drama. Also at the Traverse was *Lay By*, a show about motorway sex, or rape. Portable Theatre presented it as a satire on the sensationalist attitude of some papers to sex—very appropriate on the Fringe.

Sometimes a Fringe event could echo or complement a specific Festival emphasis. Rumanian dance was in the 1971 official programme and a troupe was brought from the

Barbara Jefford and Robin Bailey in *The Novelist* **by Tom Malin. Traverse 1971 Fringe**

same country to the Richard Demarco Gallery in Melville Crescent. The *Scotsman* review quoted below is a good example of how international the Fringe was becoming and how it could inform and educate critics:

> Two Rumanian dancers, Miriam Raducanu and Gheorghe Caciuleanu perform some of the most extraordinary dances it has ever been my privilege to see.
>
> I have never seen dancing quite like it. Except very occasionally it does not have the grace and fluidity we associate with western dance. Rather it is continually broken up by jerks of the body, the head, the arms and feet, all very angular and staccato, but done to the rhythms of heart-rending intensity.
>
> The most passionate, striking examples are given in dances to Rumanian music played and sung by peasants. In 'Cries of Longing' a lonely woman longs for her absent husband and Miriam Raducanu expresses her anguish in dance arched and contorted by pain. 'Lament', a song of grief at a burial, has the same still simplicity but is devastatingly moving.
>
> But the programme, played out against white walls with the audience squatting on the floor, is extremely varied. 'Song of Merrymaking' is complete burlesque, with accentuatedly mechanical gestures and movement, like a Rumanian version of the Marx Brothers.
>
> Similarly 'I lost my head' to a song by Adamo, and 'Minuet' to a piece by Lalo Schrifin was hilariously funny. On the other hand, 'Genesis' to a solo flute astounds us by the simplicity of gesture: hands flickeringly emerge from the neck of a dress pulled over Miss Raducanu's head. This extraordinary, eclectic programme is one of the high-spots of the Fringe.

Elizabeth Maclennan and Victor Henry in *Trees in the Wind,* **by John McGrath. This was 7:84 Theatre Company's first production, and it was done at the 1971 Fringe in the Cranston Street Hall**

In addition to new forms in drama and dance in this period there was a new element in press coverage of the Fringe in 1971. This was *Infringe*, a daily news sheet produced by Edinburgh University students and published by their Publications Board at Buccleuch Place. It later became a weekly paper and finally in the last three years, *Festival Times*. Its format has become increasingly professional and its circulation has reached 10,000 which, for a one-off publication, is remarkable. Its content is variable in standard but *Festival Times* does provide a platform for non-establishment comment with its only vested interest being controversiality. For that reason its judgement can be uncomfortably near to the mark.

 # 7:84 Theatre Company

Trevor Griffiths' *Apricots* provided another example of the 1971 Fringe's predeliction with sex. It was about a marriage in the final throes of breakup and amongst other things it involved an apricot scented vagina and the buggery of a woman. Along with John McGrath's *Trees in the Wind*, it was the first production by the 7:84 Theatre Company. They performed at the Cranston Street Hall, where Tom Stoppard's *Rosencrantz and Guildenstern Are Dead* had been premiered six years previously by the Oxford Theatre Group, who in 1959 had done John McGrath's *Why the Chicken?* McGrath formed his company to bring theatre to working-class people and gave it its distinctive name from the statistic that 7% of the population owns 84% of the country's wealth. It was based in London for the first two years of its life before splitting in 1973 into 7:84 England and 7:84 Scotland. Best equipped to outline the aims of the company is its founder, John McGrath and here is what he wrote in 1976:

There are now two different kinds of theatre in Scotland—different not necessarily in subject-matter, or even in style, but different in their attitudes to style and subject, and different in the audiences they are seeking to entertain.

One kind of theatre is dedicated to its patrons, the mainly middle-class theatre goers. It presents them with a varied fare of plays—great classics of the past, or new plays which will confirm the values of that audience about life today. Occasionally it will question those values, provide those audiences with 'food for thought'. The working class, when it appears in this kind of theatre, is an alien object, to be explained, patronised with sentimentality or laughed at. Very rarely to be taken seriously.

The other kind of theatre, which 7:84 has done a great deal to establish, is there to present the realities of working class life and history directly to working class audiences. Without translating it into the language of the middle class 'theatre' that has dominated our stages since the 1890s. It has its roots in the popular tradition of entertainment, and it takes the values of the working class very seriously.

The Scottish 7:84 Theatre Company is proud to belong to this other kind of theatre. In our three and a half years, we have put on shows about the history of the people of the Highlands from the time of the Clearances to the present day; about John MacLean, the great pioneer socialist; about the twin pressures on Highland people today of the land-ownership situation and the oil boom; about the great days of the Red Clyde and the new aspirations of the SNP; about the history of the people of Dumbarton; about the presence of the USA and its role in Scotland; and about the lives of ordinary people in the industrial areas of Scotland now.

We have used forms of entertainment that our audiences are familiar with; the ceilidh, the variety show, the concert party, music hall, band shows, the musical play have all been used as the basis from which different styles and techniques have emerged and been developed as forms of theatre.

And our audiences have been found in village halls, community centres, town halls, technical colleges, miners clubs, trades council clubs, civic centres, even an auction room, as well as in the theatres; where of course we are happy to perform if we are not expected to conform to the 'artistic' values of the current trend in middle class culture.

Inevitably we talk politics: because it is a reality of life today. And because theatre is about the way people relate to each other—and that is conditioned by economic structures, from which spring social structures, like classes and cultural patterns, like educational systems, religion and the customary relationship between the sexes. Any theatre that concentrates on 'emotional' plots and does not question the structure that underlie its characters' lives is being political by default. We choose to examine political issues openly because they shape the reality we all live in. That reality is not static and accepted—it is dynamic and in the process of change. If it is to change in a way that will make living better, then an open, clear analysis is needed. We hope that our kind of theatre can make a contribution to the way the Scottish working class decides its own future— and on the way give people 'some good theatre, some enjoyable music, a few laughs and a good night out'.

Two points emerge from McGrath's statement; first that 7:84's technique of doing temporary theatre is derived right out of Edinburgh Fringe techniques learned in 1971, and second that taking theatre to the mass of the people is what the Fringe had been doing for ten years, but only for three weeks in the year.

 # The Pool Lunch Hour Theatre Club 1971 to 1974

Like John McGrath, the founders of the Pool Lunch Hour Theatre Club were aiming to attract a different audience to their shows. Office workers and businessmen who might never think of spending an evening at the theatre might like to have a lunchbreak with a difference—a short play.

Phil Emanuel, an actor/director with the Bradford Art College Theatre Group at the 1970 Fringe, came back up to Edinburgh later that year with the idea of starting up a lunchtime theatre. Only in London were there theatres catering for a daytime trade. Emanuel went to talk with John Gray, Chief Assistant at BBC Radio Scotland, about the feasibility of his project. They found suitable premises at 76 Hanover Street and together with John Cumming, a stage technician from Edinburgh and Lindsay Levy, a writer, began working to build the theatre. 76 Hanover Street was an enormous three storey building: the ground floor incorporated a foyer where exhibitions could be mounted, a fair-sized performance area seating sixty, a room for serving lunch and coffee, and dressing rooms. The middle and top floors included a large room where Lindsay Kemp set up a studio where he gave classes in dance and mime.

Tickets for shows were fixed at 30p, and that included lunch which would be a sandwich and an orange. The audience could eat during the show. Emanuel and his partners called the theatre *The Other Pool Synod Hall*, a strange joke referring to a cinema which stood on the famous Castle Terrace site. The reference did not withstand the test of time and the theatre came to be known simply as the *Pool*. The inaugural production was on 1 February 1971 and it was Lindsay Kemp's *Turquoise Pantomime*

The whole enterprise was built on shaky foundations from the start. Emanuel had only £100 as capital, and that was the first month's rental for the building. They were utterly dependent on the box office to keep going. Fortunately the response was good—as it should have been from a public that had been exposed to so many Festivals and Fringes. The Scottish Arts Council came quickly to the Pool's aid with an initial grant of £500 in its first year, and a fair amount of support thereafter.

At its first Fringe in 1971 the Pool aimed to establish itself with international audiences and critics, as well as introducing itself to London theatre critics, much as the Traverse had done in 1963. The Pool's programme was huge with shows starting at midday and the last production coming down at 1.15 am. Phil Emanuel had definite views about the Fringe and the role of his theatre in it. *Infringe* reported,

> Their ideas for the Festival were slightly different: they thought that the Fringe was dying because not enough people were doing new things and far too many Fringe shows are just ego-trips for over-grown school play starlets. Their solution was to bring up as many professional groups as possible whose work they knew and admired; groups with something to give like Theatre of Cruelty, Portable Theatre, Soho Theatre from London, and the John Bull Puncture Repair Kit, Bradford College of Art and the Welfare State from the Yorkshire area. They put on six shows a day including a kids show (Theatre Workshop Edinburgh), folk music, lunchtime and late night plays.
>
> And they have been successful: good audiences and good responses from public and critics.

While this passage shows how completely Emanuel had failed to grasp the nature of the Fringe, its openness availed his theatre much. The Pool was put on the map and its strong Fringe performance, against probably the stiffest competition outside London at that time, persuaded the Scottish Arts Council to grant the Pool a further £1000 to cover the coming six months.

As with the early days of the Traverse, the Pool staggered from financial crisis to financial crisis. After a year it desperately needed £8000 to carry on. By June 1972 the Arts Council had come up with £5250, the Gulbenkian Foundation with £2000 and the Edinburgh Corporation gave £250, its first support of the Pool.

All in all 1972 was probably the Pool's best year. they had sufficient funds to improve their premises and audiences seemed to be building up to what turned out for them another prestigious Fringe—probably the most adventurous mounted by Emanuel and Cumming. They staged their own 'International Festival' with companies from Argentina, Holland, Israel, Japan and the USA. In addition there were leading British companies like Pip Simmons Theatre Group, Ken Campbell Road Show, the John Bull Puncture Repair Kit and the Bradford Art College Theatre Group. To accommodate this wealth of Fringe talent, they opened the top floor at 76 Hanover Street.

The Pool kept up its standards outside Festival-time, too; Allen Wright in *The Scotsman* of 7 July 1972—

> The Pool looks so much more inviting than it did a few weeks ago that many people will be tempted to take the plunge. The front of Edinburgh's lunch hour theatre in Hanover Street has been renovated, and the sweet smell of success pervaded the premises when they reopened yesterday.
>
> Jack Gerson's *Ladies in Waiting* was greeted with loud laughter and prolonged applause from the largest audience I have seen in the Pool. This comedy of Morningside manners is so beautifully played by Jean Faulds and Jan Wilson that it deserves to have full houses every day.
>
> It is easy for playwrights to make fun of frustrated ladies and their romantic fantasies, but

Gerson takes a kindly view of this autocratic widow and her dowdy companion-housekeeper. Their dreams about the man upstairs cause tensions between them but ultimately draws them closer together.

Miss Faulds gives an impression of monumental smugness, smothering her meek companion. This could be a bourgeois version of Lady Bracknell. The opening scene at the dinner table is particularly enjoyable. Scolding her companion for loitering over the shopping, she asks if she has been looking for a man: 'It is not a crime to meet a man,' thunders Miss Faulds, 'but it would be a great inconvenience to me.'

It is a formidable but amusing study of selfishness and self-righteousness and Miss Wilson's gentle portrait of the crushed subordinate is also engaging. The setting is as genteel as the characters and Phil Emanuel's production is authentic in every detail.

Emanuel and his partner, John Cumming, have stocked the Pool with a wide range of entertainment. Even if it is seldom avant-garde, it is always enterprising.

After the 1973 Fringe when the Pool again had an overflowing programme, including its most successful production, Hector MacMillan's *The Sash*, Phil Emanuel left his job as Director. His enthusiasm for the idea of the Pool (apparently he once lay in the pavement outside the theatre feigning rigor mortis with rigid arm pointing to the door of the Pool) and the sheer audacity in starting it at all, are qualities Edinburgh should be grateful for.

His successor was John Abulafia, a writer and director. Unfortunately, the Pool was forced to leave 76 Hanover Street because the building was to be 'redeveloped' i.e. pulled down. This really spelt the downfall of the whole enterprise. Hanover Street was the perfect location to accommodate the office workers in the New Town. It was on a main thoroughfare and the space inside was very handy. For most of 1974 the Pool's committee looked in vain for a suitable venue while productions went on at the YWCA in Randolph Place and the Crown Theatre, Edinburgh University Drama Society's building in Hill Place, off Nicholson Street.

For the 1974 Fringe the Pool used the Cranston Street Hall and the building which now houses the Edinburgh Wax Museum at 142 High Street. Amongst a host of premieres, was John Abulafia's *Drumbuie Faustus* which dealt with the attempts of John Mowlem and Taylor Woodrow to build drilling rigs in the tiny Highland village. Using the images of Marlowe's play, Abulafia constructed a powerful political argument against the rape of the tiny community of Drumbuie for the sake of only fifteen years of use. Perhaps the show helped in the struggle to fight off the advances of these powerful companies.

Also appearing were the Artaud Company, who had really begun life at the Pool in 1972 with the play, *Monsieur Artaud*. They did *Letters from K*, a double bill written and directed by Michael Almaz. It was about Franz Kafka, his life and a young woman whom he first courted and then rejected.

Sadly this was to be the Pool's last Fringe. In February 1975 the theatre's Chairman, John Gray, promised that the debts amounting to more than £3000 would be paid. He counted on 'the goodwill many people felt towards the Pool' to contribute the cash needed to wind up affairs honourably.

While it existed the Pool provided another permanent Fringe theatre in Edinburgh which operated all the year round, and it provided a fresh professional focus for the Fringe. It is missed and, although attempts have been made to raise cash to resurrect it, it seems likely that nothing will come of them. The tragedy is that the Pool did not fade away through lack of support but because, once deprived of its premises at 76 Hanover Street, alternative accommodation could not be found—surprising in a city which throws up 97 theatre spaces for the Fringe.

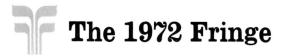# The 1972 Fringe

As John Milligan began to exert his considerable administrative talents, the Fringe became in every way more popular. In the first week of the 1972 Fringe the box office passed the total sales for the entire Fringe in 1971. The Fringe Club was enjoying its first year in the Royal Mile Centre, a suite of bars and function rooms in the High Street—in a prime position between the Tron Kirk and St Giles Cathedral. Because it is an intimate building and not a series of elegant, barn-like rooms like the Festival Club in George Street, the Royal Mile Centre makes an excellent Fringe Club. With the groups themselves providing what must be the most varied cabaret in the world, cheap and good food at all hours and a late licence to 1.30 am every night, the Fringe Club has a huge membership of both public and performers. They patronise it constantly and it is, for three weeks, the most entertaining and exciting place in the city. As such it is largely John Milligan's achievement.

Turning to finance, Milligan's temporary appointment in 1971 had blossomed into a full-time job by 1972. The Fringe Society had become a viable economic proposition with grants from the Edinburgh Corporation (£1000) and, at last, from the Scottish Arts Council, also £1000. The number of groups had risen as Milligan had found more spaces for them to perform in and as the Society had developed expertise in publicising the Fringe collectively. Patrick Brooks, one of the most committed of the voluntary workers in the Sixties, admitted that 'without John Milligan the task would have been impossible this year. The Fringe has completely outgrown the scope of the voluntary organisation.'

However, not everyone was pleased with the new professionalism in the running of the Society. Michael Walker of the Oxford Theatre Group had complaints:

> It has become too easy for groups to join in, with ready-made promotional support through their membership of the Society. The groups taking part have doubled in number in two years, and you get a lot of dead wood on the Fringe.
>
> The other point is that many are regarding this Fringe as a place to call on tour. They are presenting shows they have done with success elsewhere, rather than bringing new material. They just come here to be loved and to play safe.

Everybody needs to be loved, including Walker's Oxford Theatre Group. The problem for many groups was that they did not have Oxford's experience in courting affection with the public. The Fringe Society simply gave good advice as to how to go about this. All the points raised by Walker were seen by the public as worthwhile developments, and he was wrong about new work. There were 45 premiere productions in the 1972 Fringe, more than there had ever been before.

Contrasting with or perhaps following on from sex as the theme of the 1971 Fringe, politics was the subject of many plays in 1972. Locations ranged from Glasgow, to Ireland to Dallas, Texas.

An American actress, Patricia Gilbert, did a one-woman show *The Assassination of President Kennedy*. She recreated the event by looking at it through the eyes of the women directly involved; Jackie Kennedy, Ladybird Johnson, Mrs John Connally and Mrs Oswald. By doing this, Miss Gilbert could evoke the excitement of the Kennedy administration and the idealism it inspired—in an atmosphere (in 1972) in which the whole Kennedy myth had been rejected. She even succeeded in converting the reviewer from *Infringe*.

A scene from *The Great Northern Welly Boot Show*

More hard-edged in its approach was *The Ballygombeen Bequest* by John Arden and Margaretta D'Arcy, performed by the 7:84 Theatre Company. Its subject was absentee landlords in southern Ireland and their effect. The action of the play parallels real events and real villains and victims. The audience were asked to sign a petition at the theatre protesting about the removal of squatters' right by landlords, often seeking to create holiday homes for tourists by evicting their Irish occupants. Although not rapturously reviewed the show did much to establish 7:84 as a company who could confront live issues with their theatrical talents and thereby cause their audiences to be concerned and thoughtful.

The Great Northern Welly Boot Show takes a more humourous but nonetheless concerned look at the Upper Clyde Shipyard work-in. It was written by Tom McGrath and Billy Connolly and it enjoyed a huge success with most performances being sold out—which is surprising considering it was done in the vast Waverley Market. The show deals with the shutdown of the Clydeside Welly Boot Company as a result of managerial incompetence, its takeover by the workers who are resolved to keep the welly boot industry afloat. The final twist in the drama is the intervention of an American firm who buy the company. Michael Billington reviewed the show:

> No-one could call the show politically profound. The bosses are agitprop cutouts with fat paunches and cigars; all Tories and media men are languid and effete; all the workers muscular and good-hearted. Yet the show is sustained first by a driving, angry conviction that Scotland has been turned into an economic disaster area by successive English politicians; and secondly by its application of all the elements of pop theatre (song and dance, pier-end comedy, music

and above all earthiness) to a serious end. There is even a stunning striptease performed to beaming, giant-sized carnival caricatures of Wilson and Heath. We constantly bleat about the absence of a genuine popular theatre in Britain; well here it is. And what's more it's attracting a local audience rather than the usual collection of visiting culture vultures.

El Coca Cola Grande was the title of a revue-style show done by the Low Moan Spectacular in the Edinburgh University Union. The action takes place in a Central American night club run by a well known Nicaraguan compere, Pepe Hernandez. The entertainment was provided by his family posing as internationally famous cabaret acts. The whole thing was done in a kind of pidgin Spanish/English. Low Moan had already been reviewed in London but what they were hoping for in Edinburgh was attention from American critics, so that they could negotiate a transfer to the US. At the Fringe it all happened for them. Early in 1973 El Coca Cola Grande opened at Joe Papp's Public Theater in New York's Lower East Side before moving to a larger space in Greenwich village. The show ran for two years.

There were more than 100 performing groups at the 1972 Fringe not counting 20 exhibitions. This dramatic rise in numbers probably made the Edinburgh Festival as a whole the largest festival in the world. This was a direct result of John Milligan's efficiency and growing expertise.

 # 'The Scotsman' Fringe Firsts 1973 to 1977

The 1972 Fringe had contained 45 new plays and in the main these had not been amongst the most successful at the box office. The Fringe programme had become so big and mind-boggling that audiences were prone to search through for the familiar, preferring the tried and trusted revivals or the groups with established reputations to a chancy evening out with a premiere by an unknown group. Very conscious of this trend and the traditional role of the Fringe as a platform for new work, the Fringe Board, on the advice of groups attending the 1972 Annual General Meeting, determined to find a way of encouraging those willing to take the risk of doing a new play. After rejecting a revival of the old Scottish Union of Students Trophy (which had been given to the best Student venture on the Fringe), the Board decided to approach *The Scotsman* with the idea of a scheme whereby they should review all new work and give awards to the best. Ian Thomson, from the Publicity Department and Allen Wright, the arts editor, collaborated with John Milligan to produce *The Scotsman* Fringe Firsts Scheme.

The definition of a Fringe First came from Allen Wright. The awards would go to companies doing world and British premieres of plays and dance pieces, excluding revue material and allowing for preview performances outside Edinburgh. In 1977 up to six preview performances were allowed so that the show could be properly run in before the Fringe. In the words of Allen Wright, the awards were to be given for 'enterprise and originality'.

So, in 1973 teams of *Scotsman* reviewers went out into the field to seek out the outstanding new work on the Fringe. If any of them came back really raving about a show, Wright sent out another critic in order to get a second opinion. If both critics agreed, the show was given a *Scotsman* Fringe First. The award itself is a rather attractive copper plaque inscribed with the name of its winner.

**Pilobolus Dance Theatre,
U.S.A. at the 1973 Fringe**

Initially, in 1973, only ten Firsts were given but later as quality and quantity grew as many as fourteen could be awarded. There is a complete list of all the winners in Appendix A (page 120).

In all there have been 52 awards made (sadly only six amateur companies have received one) out of 442 plays and dance pieces which have had their premieres on the Fringe since 1973. There can be no doubt that the *Scotsman* awards have stimulated much of this creativity since the total of new works has risen from 49 in 1973 to 138 in 1977. More new plays and dance pieces are done in three weeks in Edinburgh than are done in the West End in an entire year. That fact alone makes the Fringe one of the most important festivals in the English-speaking world. It acts as a lifeline of new writing talent for the theatre much more directly than it helps performers to be noticed or stimulated.

 # Administration 1973 to 1975

Between 1973 and 1975 the Edinburgh Fringe grew considerably. Its audience was barely able to keep pace: as the number of performances rose so did the size of the total audience. The average house, however, stayed at around 60 all through this period:

> 1973—87 performing groups did 1386 performances for 42,990 seats
> 1974—115 performing groups did 1645 performances for 54,539 seats
> 1975—123 performing groups did 1971 performances for 62,483 seats

If you divide the number of performances into the number of seats sold at the central Fringe box office, you will get a quotient of thirty. Actual curtain-up figures are reckoned to be thrice that since the groups sell tickets at the door before performances. This does not seem a large figure unless you remember that most Fringe halls only seat 100 or so.

Ultimately what these figures indicate is that the market for the performing arts in Edinburgh at Festival time is not finite and can expand as the amount of entertainment on offer expands. Significantly the number of Fringe tickets sold in 1974 was more than were sold for official shows. That has continued to be the case ever since.

In order to cope with its success the Fringe Society had to improve its services to the public and the groups. Milligan first turned his attention to the publications. In March 1973 he brought out the usual Preliminary Handbill listing those groups who were definitely coming at that stage, and he increased its circulation—20,000 were printed and distributed nationwide and occasionally (when a cheap way of doing it could be found) overseas. The Handbill was simply a list with only the names of the groups and their shows on it, but it did awaken interest and increase the volume of requests for the full detailed Fringe Programme which came out in late June.

The 1973 Programme was really a model exercise in compressing information into a cheap and very readable format. It looked like a four-page newspaper printed on good quality art paper: the programme information was on one side with *The Scotsman* premieres on the other side along with the map, Milligan's introduction and the list of services available. 50,000 were published in June and an updated reprint of 28,000 in August.

The information as presented in the programme was a little bald. It did not give the groups any space to say much about themselves or their shows, and it left the public with difficult decisions about new shows or groups that did not have a reputation. The Fringe Brochure was first produced as an additional guide to the Fringe in 1972. In 1973 it became a pocket-size booklet of 128 pages selling at 25p. Each group was given a page to

Pucka Ri. **A rock musical based on Celtic mythology at the 1973 Fringe**

say what it liked about itself and its shows. They are encouraged to give hard information although some took the view that the Brochure page should carry photographic material which was absent from the Programme. All in all the publication helped to show the diversity of attitudes on the Fringe.

From the work of the Administrator to his Board of Directors, the Fringe's policy-making body: the Board had been without a Chairman since the death of Lord Grant in a car accident in November 1972. George Shaw had taken over temporarily and the Board were fortunate enough to have the services of Mike Westcott for the latter part of 1973. Finally Westcott, Milligan and Andrew Kerr met Andrew Cruickshank in Glasgow to offer him the Chairmanship. Happily he accepted and since 1974 Cruickshank has given to the Fringe the length and breadth of his experience in the theatre. And, in a sense, he has given the Fringe to his profession with an evangelical fervour. He believes in the Fringe as a lifeline of new talent to the theatre, and as a unique form of arts organisation which ought to be exported more widely than it is.

The Fringe's Board is intended to represent the interests of the groups who participate. At present there are representatives of Cambridge Footlights, Nottingham Theatre Group, Atit, Boundstone School, Middleton St George College of Education, Swindon College Drama Unit, Strathclyde Theatre Group, the University of Edinburgh and finally, Richard Crane and Faynia Williams who, up until this year, ran the University of Bradford Drama Group. As can be seen from the list of Fringe Firsts, Bradford have been one of the most consistently successful groups in the Seventies.

Birkenhead Dada. This group appeared in 1973 and the photograph conveys their message adequately

Performances 1973 to 1975

Richard Crane had been involved both as an actor and a writer with the Pool before he wrote and directed *Thunder*, Bradford's first big production on the Fringe. A play about the Brontës, it was a sober and sensitive reconstruction of the atmosphere at Haworth, using episodes from the novels of Charlotte, Emily and Anne to illustrate the fantasies and frustrations of the sisters. The following year Chris Parr directed *The Quest* also by Richard Crane. Michael Billington reviewed the show in *The Guardian*,

> I have long suspected that the attraction of the Arthurian legend is that you can make it mean almost anything you like . . . Richard Crane uses it to illustrate the dangers of a privileged elitism that ignores the realities of common life.
>
> I think the work with its hymns-ancient-and-modern style music by Chris Mitchell and spectacular direction by Chris Parr is a stunning achievement; and not least because it builds everything around a simple linguistic contrast. Arthur wants to create a kingdom based on moderation, truth and justice; but its outward symbol is less the Round Table than his determination that everyone speak in verse.
>
> Mordred becomes the leader of the underprivileged prose speakers and in so doing reveals that Camelot, under its verbal splendour, is riddled with rancour, deception and lies.
>
> On one level the piece is an action spectacular, drawing on Mallory, Tennyson, and 'Sir Gawaine and the Green Knight', on another it is a topical political parable about the nature of good government and the danger of letting a fractious warring elite make decisions without reference to popular needs. But what gives it the kick is its sheer theatrical panache; the stage area is a long narrow strip in which the rival parties become sporting contestants ('Come on Arthur,' the woman behind me shouted, as if cheering on Rangers).
>
> It is, in fact, the ideal work for a university company on the Edinburgh Fringe; formal surroundings and a high professional gloss could kill it. But Mr Parr's direction is very precise (his sound effects are thunderously right) and there are more than useful performances from John Lamb as a head-in-the-sand Arthur, and from Jenny Roebuck as a fickle flirt of Guinevere. Brecht always wanted a theatre that resembled the sporting events: well here it is.

The actress who played Lady Bellicent in *The Quest* was Faynia Williams. She directed the next Crane/Bradford show *Clownmaker*, a play which explored the relationship between Diaghilev and the dancer, Nijinsky. The former as cold and ruthless manipulator, the latter as the trapped puppet. Faynia Williams' eye for pictorially effective direction was noted by the reviewers and it was exactly that talent that provided one of the major reasons for the success of Bradford's 1977 production, the magnificent *Satan's Ball*.

Having taken 1976 off (to go to perform in Poland) Crane and Williams (by this time Crane and Crane—they were married during the 1975 Fringe) released details of the new show in early August saying, amongst much else, that *Satan's Ball* would include a scene with Christ crucified naked. Sadly *The Sunday Mail* picked on this titbit and blew it up into a front page story with comments from religious leaders and Mrs Mary Whitehouse about a play which none of them had seen. Yet another 'filthy Fringe' smear which, in the event, the splendours of *Satan's Ball* banished as soon as the play opened.

Like *The Quest* this play exploited the space it found itself in—the old university Chaplaincy Centre. The photographs in the appendix show the stages of construction but they cannot capture the fluidity of Williams's direction as the action moved between the three levels, seemingly suspended in mid air through a subtle use of lighting. Some of the scenes where all three levels and the floor were in use were so well co-ordinated that when the action paused, they seemed like set-pieces, carefully constructed tableaux-vivants. *Satan's Ball* also existed on many historical levels—Crane obviously enjoys using the past (or legend) to point up problems of the present—Pontius Pilate and his dealings with Christ and contrasted with life in Soviet Russia and their reaction to a visit from Satan who plans a ball. The play must rank as one of the most splendid events of the 1977 Fringe; just as *Carmen* in the 1977 official Festival seemed to sum up what Festivals are about so *Satan's Ball* could be seen as the very stuff of Fringes.

In contrast with the size of the Bradford operation is Russell Hunter's series of very popular one-man shows in this period. He began with *Cocky* in 1970, a play about Edinburgh's Lord Cockburn. *Jock*, possibly Hunter's most successful show, followed in 1972. It was written by W. Gordon Smith as a one-man examination of the Scots' attitude to themselves using the character of a sergeant in a Highland regiment as a vehicle. Religion, the Scottish inferiority complex, the fierce patriotism, even our carbohydrate-ridden diet all make the archetypal—but never predictable—Scotsman that Hunter creates on stage. Gordon Smith went further than simple outlining the symptoms of Scottishness: he tried to use *Jock* to investigate the reasons why there's nane like us. On a minimal stage setting with a barrage of props, Hunter used all his strength and theatrical guile to rant and cajole the audience into seeing *Jock*'s point of view. Hunter and Smith attracted audiences from all quarters and, because of the simple nature of the show, were able to tour it around Scotland. This was drama about Scotland of the best sort—with far more to say to Scots than some of admittedly funny or nostalgic Scots drama which one sees on the Fringe.

Hunter and Smith concentrated on one aspect of the Scots make-up—religion, when they premiered *Knox* in 1974. The Reformer was portrayed as a fearless servant of God who was ultimately responsible for much that was bad in present-day Scotland—the deathly Scottish Sunday, the hypocritical sanctimoniousness of some Presbyterians and so on. Knox's pulpit becomes a dock as he accused by many characters, all played by Derek Anders and Mary Ann Reid. Like *Jock*, *Knox* was enormously successful and like *The Great Northern Welly Boot Show*, it attracted a predominantly Scottish audience.

The costumes for *Knox* were designed by an Edinburgh artist, Edith Simon. She has exhibited her work regularly on the Fringe. In 1973 at the Old Chaplaincy Centre she did the Edith Simon Adventure Show, a group of works in many media. This was 'total art' which involved people in not only looking at sculptures or paintings but also made them reconsider everyday objects because of the way in which the artist had treated them. Edith Simon also has an incurable sense of fun which you can see in the armchair on page 103. Her exhibitions show that the initiative in this side of the Edinburgh Fringe does not always lie with Richard Demarco.

Theatre managers, agents, television drama producers and general talent-spotters have always come in numbers to the Fringe. If a new show takes off in this most competitive of festivals then it must have a lot going for it, enough to carry it to London's West End or on to television screens. *Shylock* was a rock musical by Paul Bentley and Roger Haynes. It was done in a small church hall in Johnston Terrace, near the Castle. The hall could only have seated about 90 people and the playing area was tiny. But it was this special brand of Fringe intimacy and the fact that the actors and musicians had to create the show out of very little under such close scrutiny which gave *Shylock* its charge. The show was a runaway success and the winner of a Fringe First. The production impressed Ray Cooney, a London impresario, and he bought it. Three years and many rewrites later, a blown-up version of *Shylock* appeared in the West End as *Fire Angel*. It was a disaster. The critics hated it just as they had loved *Shylock*, and it closed after a few weeks and the loss of a

This armchair appeared in the Edith Simon exhibition at the 1973 Fringe

sizeable investment. The point to make is that *Shylock* was a product of the Fringe and it should have stayed there. West End commercial-type theatre is a different genre needing shows which can have a large impact or are written in a conventional style which sits easily in a big theatre.

Perri St Claire and George Logan had developed a revue-style act as Dame Hilda Bracket and Doctor Evadne Hinge, or just Hinge and Bracket. Their programme notes give an idea of their show:

> Doctor Evadne Hinge and her lifelong friend and partner Dame Hilda Bracket have journeyed to Edinburgh from their home in Stackton Tressel to bring a little culture to the Festival Fringe.
>
> They will be performing some of their favourite songs from the works of Gilbert and Sullivan; some you don't know, some you may not, and others they don't quite know themselves.

They enjoyed great popular success, which led to a Scottish Arts Council tour, which led eventually to great things in show business. The Fringe gave them the sort of publicity they needed. In contrast with *Shylock*, Hinge and Bracket was a pure showbiz venture that lost nothing in the translation.

In addition to musical shows, the Fringe was able to offer four operas in 1974. *Hugh Miller* was the only full-length one to be done by professionals. The libretto by Colin MacLean, then Editor of the Times Educational Supplement Scotland, told the story of Miller, a stonemason who also had an interest in geology. He was a prolific pamphleteer and author, his most popular book being *Old Redsandstones* which at the time outsold Darwin's *Origin of the Species*. In 1834 Miller moved to Edinburgh to become a bank accountant—to please his social-climbing wife, and was asked to edit the Evangelical Party's new newspaper, *The Witness*. This embroiled him in the Disruption of the Church of Scotland, a doctrinal dispute which raged in 1843. Miller was eventually driven by the pressures of his marriage to commit suicide at Portobello in 1856.

The composer of the opera, Reginald Barrett-Ayres, wrote a score which reflected the subject and the period: strathspeys, metrical psalms and traditional songs. Miller's life was treated in a series of tableaux describing important incidents. The production was done in St Giles Cathedral, possibly the most appropriate setting available anywhere.

Hugh Miller provides an example of the artistic breadth of the Fringe Programme and of how the Fringe can encompass shows with something new and cogent to say about Scotland and its history. Along with much of the new work being done at the Pool and the Traverse, and Gordon Smith's one-man shows for Russell Hunter, *Hugh Miller* should be seen as part of the growth of Scottish drama about Scotland which has taken place in the Seventies.

In contrast with this optimism, efforts by the Fringe Society to make theatre itself more popular with the majority of Scots have not been entirely successful. John Milligan believed that all classes of people could enjoy theatre and that the Fringe might be the sort of informal vehicle to bring it to them. With the help of Jack Kane, Edinburgh's only Labour Lord Provost, Milligan organised venues in the largely council-estate suburbs of Pilton, Craigmillar, Sighthill, Portobello, Firhill and Gilmerton. Before the Festival began eight companies did their previews in the suburbs and audiences stayed away in droves. Although the scheme was revived each year until it faded out in 1976, it never really caught on.

The Seventies saw a notable increase in foreign entries to the Fringe. From the United States came the San Quentin Drama Workshop with their much-travelled production *The Cage*. The author, Rick Cluchey, and the actors had all been inmates of San Quentin and the drama centres around their experiences in jail. The point of the play is to show that a prolonged period of imprisonment is more likely to deprave and corrupt than cure.

Dancers Anonymous are a group
of young dancers formed by
Bridget Crowley to appear at the
Edinburgh Fringe each year. They
have been coming to perform
since 1974 when this photograph
was taken

From *After Brecht* by Freies
Theatre Munchen in 1974

Violence, homosexuality and insanity form the keynotes of life in San Quentin and this was brought out without equivocation. However, when the play was performed for prisoners at Saughton Prison in Edinburgh, they were not impressed and felt that 'it lets prisoners down'. Nevertheless the incident did stimulate interest in drama at Saughton and a workshop was started.

Also from America came Tommy Taylor with his one-man show *Woody Guthrie, Child of Dust*. He entered the Fringe Programme at the last minute but the Society was able to promote him sufficiently for his show to be successful. John Barber's review, however, hints at one of the most powerful forms of advertising on the Fringe, word of mouth.

> Amazing how the word gets around. News of something exceptional is cramming Edinburgh's Lodge Canongate Kilwinning. Young people of all nationalities are eager to catch the unknown Tommy Taylor's one-man *Woody Guthrie, Child of Dust*.
>
> For Guthrie, chronicler of the dust-bowl depression era in the 1930s, and a balladeer who influenced Bob Dylan, is acknowledged as a true American original.
>
> Mr Taylor, a shy graduate from Texas, far more cultured than you might suppose from his nasal, folksy twang, has spent 10 years accumulating the material for his show.
>
> Guthrie comes across as a hickory-wood philosopher in the Mark Twain–Will Rogers tradition. As a boy, he learned to play the harmonica from an Oklahoma shoeshine boy. As a youth he peddled root whisky so strong it blew your shirt buttons off.
>
> As a man, he devised words and music to tell how 300,000 people went to California to escape winds that blew the barbs from barbed-wire fences, and storms like the ocean jumping on a snail.
>
> His songs, hard-bitten but not bitter, are sung in a relaxed style by Mr Taylor. I found some of the religious homilies hard to take, and the fulsome praise of trade unions even harder. But these are period documents and the lyrics have the good smell of the open air.
>
> After the interval, the ballads of social protest give way to Guthrie's unexpected songs for children.

Expansion and a Permanent Home 1976 and 1977

John Milligan resigned as Administrator of the Fringe Society after the 1975 Festival. He had spent five productive years shaping the structure of the Society and, to use his own phrase, 'honing up its expertise'. Milligan's reasons for leaving were straightforward enough. He felt that he had given as much as he could to the Fringe and that it needed the fresh influence of a new Administrator.

The Board appointed Alistair Moffat, a graduate of St Andrews and London universities, as the new Administrator. Although his experience of running an office was slight, Moffat had been involved in starting the first St Andrews Festival and had been director and founder of a small annual arts festival in his native town of Kelso.

The policy decisions for the 1976 Fringe had already been taken and Moffat's role was to learn and operate the existing structure of the Society for his first year. His immediate influence was seen in the huge increase in the number of participating groups for 1976. The total of 182 performing groups was 60 more than had participated in the 1975 Fringe. Of all the groups who made the trip to Edinburgh before the Festival in order to find a hall, almost all were successful because Moffat had found 19 new spaces willing to let to

Tommy Taylor in *Woody Guthrie, Child of Dust*, **1975**

the Fringe. Despite this rise in the numbers of shows, total ticket sales fell slightly compared with the previous year. For 2928 performances 59,120 seats were sold.

There were, however, three encouraging signs. First, the standard of performances was probably at its highest ever with fourteen Fringe Firsts being awarded. Second, coverage of the event from press and broadcasting was better than it had ever been. And third, a survey of the economic impact of the whole Festival gave some hard information about the size of the total Fringe audience and where they came from. The survey, done by Roger Vaughn of the Heriot Watt University, showed that curtain-up audiences at Fringe shows can be reckoned as, on average, triple the number of tickets sold at the central box office. So, when 72,649 tickets were sold at the Fringe box office in 1977, the total number of tickets sold for Fringe shows would be in the region of 220,000.

Returning to the 1976 Fringe as arguably the best ever, artistically, there seemed to be an emphasis, like sex in 1971 or politics in 1972, on fantasy. One of the best of the touring Fringe companies, Paines Plough, did the premiere of David Pownall's *Music To Murder By*. Three characters from different historical periods act out the drama; Gesualdo, a 16th-century Italian musician, Philip Heseltine, a music critic from the early part of this century who embraced the Devil and changed his name to Warlock, and an American lady whose interests are in musicology. The play forces these three levels to confront each other. And if *Music To Murder By* had a subject outside of its characters, it is contained in Gesualdo's words, 'if you wish to investigate my music you must have regard for me'. Within the play there is some superb music. In fact the look of the show was excellent, delicately beautiful.

Mockhero's Heron by Stuart Delves carried on the fantastic theme:

> A Festival is first of all a time for delight in creativity: a celebration that we too (and more particularly we two) can share in divinity. Stuart Delves is a young dramatist, this is his first play, and part of the considerable pleasure to be had comes from just this.
>
> We have four characters taken all at once from myth, fairy-tale and the everyday world, here in this great O; by games, dressing up, story-telling, role-playing, they explore the nature of reality. Mr Delves is fascinated by ideas and fertile in them. He throws out philosophical paradoxes with fine extravagance. He can create characters too. It's easy in this sort of play for the roles to become only symbols. These characters though have a solidity that comes through.
>
> A warning: the first act contains some longueurs when the language gets in the way of the play's development. The second act from a delicious mock-Rattigan opening, is a triumphant success.

> Alan Massie, *The Scotsman*

One of the most hilarious moments in the 1976 Fringe came from the Entertainment Machine from London. Their play must have the longest title ever seen in the Programme, *The Farndale Avenue Housing Estate Townswomens' Guild's Dramatic Society's Production of Macbeth*. Its subject was ham acting and some said that no more appropriate subject could be found on the Fringe.

Turning from drama to mime, 1976 proved a vintage year with Gary Shore from America, the Berne Mime Ensemble, Claire Heggen and Yves Marc and Mime Amiel. All of these played to large audiences with Amiel's brilliant one-man show taking a Fringe First. Of all the performing arts it is most noticeable that dance and mime have a strong audience in Edinburgh and they have sustained a consistently high standard of work from Fringe companies.

The growth of the Fringe was not seen as a positive step by everyone. Some critics, especially, complained that it had become too big. Cordelia Oliver wrote in *The Guardian* in 1976,

Sarah Collier as Dorothy Parker in *Dorothy and the Bitch* **by Marcella Evaristi, 1976**

Jean-Pierre Amiel in *Un Jour La Terre*, **1976**

The Edinburgh Festival Fringe grows grosser every year like a fat old cat going to seed and not giving a damn. The official Fringe programme lists at least two hundred companies of one kind or another in every available space from Craigmillar to Leith in shows which at best are capable of matching the best in the official Festival. But at its own worst—a far more common occurrence—the Fringe is bad beyond belief.

The subject splits opinion right down the middle. Some say the very essence of the Fringe is its free-for-all nature: that it's the way it grew and to try and change things is to tempt the fates. Others say nonsense, the fates were tempted long ago when the Fringe itself went official, appointed its own director and began to print its own programme of events.

So why not go further and devise some way of indicating value for ticket money: why not even appoint some trusted scout to be on the look out for unusually stimulating small groups from anywhere in the world and invite at least one to Edinburgh each year.

It is surprising to observe a critic complaining that there is too much to see, too many premieres, too much inventiveness, too much enterprise and Mrs Oliver should know that outside of the British Fringe there is not an abundance in the theatre of these characteristics. Critics can get frustrated and angry at the size of the Fringe, but mercifully most reviewers rejoice in diversity.

Towards the end of the 1976 Fringe, Stewart Boyd, the Pictures Editor of *The Scotsman*, suggested that the Fringe ought to have a symbol to identify itself apart from the Festival—on publicity, in the newspaper reviews, in its programme and so on. Ian Thomson of the Publicity department, who had been involved with the Fringe Firsts in 1973, decided that *The Scotsman* should sponsor a competition to find a symbol with the entries to be judged by Andrew Cruickshank, Alistair Moffat, Allen Wright, Stewart Boyd and himself. The winning design, by Alan Victor, a commercial artist who had also been responsible for the Film Festival's symbol, was chosen because it represented growth, the four main arts to be found on the Fringe, two Fs (the one reversed out of the other) and because it would enlarge and reduce well. There is a good example on the cover of this book, and in the frontage of the new Fringe office.

The new office was the major decision taken by the Board of Directors in 1976/77. The Fringe Society needed two things if it were to grow at the same pace as its Programme; a new year-round office and a new box office. One reason for the decline of the number of tickets sold at the central box office in 1976 was that the method of selling the tickets was so awkward. The box office was situated at the top of a stairway on the third floor of the Royal Mile Centre. The room which housed it was too small to cope efficiently and quickly with customers. The Society needed a box office that was accessible directly off the street and which could process orders faster through having more selling points and more space to handle tickets. Also the year-round Fringe office at the Royal Mile Centre was less than satisfactory. The accommodation was actually a disused pub which had a leaky roof and frequent floods, which incidentally destroyed many of the records necessary for this book. The Board resolved to look for new premises and almost immediately found them twenty yards from the Royal Mile Centre at 170 High Street. The building had been a draper's shop and it belonged to Lothian Regional Council. They agreed to let it to the Fringe Society, and the Scottish Arts Council agreed to contribute to the renovation of 170 High Street. Andrew Kerr, the Company Secretary for the Fringe carried through the complex negotiations with owners, contractors and the city authorities. A firm of Edinburgh designers, Graphic Partners, worked within the listed building regulations to produce a custom-built Fringe box office which was finished ten minutes before it opened on Wednesday 10 August.

The new box office is a handsome sight and it attracted people much more readily than

The new Fringe box office at 170 High Street

Photograph courtesy Graphic Partners

the old ad-hoc arrangements at the Royal Mile Centre. Its existence was certainly one good reason for the spectacular rise in the size of the 1977 Fringe audience. 170 High Street will now be the permanent home of the Fringe Society which had been wandering from office to office for thirty years. As with the formation of the Fringe into a limited company, the successful move to a new permanent office can be seen largely as the achievement of Andrew Kerr.

The 1977 Fringe itself was hugely successful with many, many shows receiving good reviews and sizeable audiences. Besides *Satan's Ball*, two shows caught much attention. The first of these was *Writer's Cramp* by a new playwright, John Byrne. John Bett and Alex Norton played all the characters who figured in the life and times of Francis Seneca McDade, who was played by Bill Paterson. The show contained flashes of pure genius as it traced out McDade's career as author, painter, poet and broadcaster. The programme notes bring out the humour of McDade's pitiful bourgeois pseudo-intellectualism,

> An in-depth reconstruction of the life and work of the Poet/Painter F. S. McDade, with tea and home baking provided by the Nitshill Writing Circle. Paintings kindly loaned by the Busby Sketch Club.
>
> Works like *Pass the Buns, Dolly* and *Feet of Clay* made Francis Seneca McDade the voice of a generation. In this lively Drama Documentary, McDade's unique story unfolds with enormous sympathy. Quite simply, as a Painter, Poet and human being he displayed a sense of purpose unmatched since the time of Annie S Swan. He came from near Paisley.

Like Dolls or Angels was done by the National Student Theatre Company, got together to appear at the 1977 Fringe (and it is hoped at each successive festival). John Barber of *The Daily Telegraph* thought it was a masterpiece:

> The Fringe of the Edinburgh Festival is a forcing house for new talent. It fostered Jonathan Miller, the director. It produced Tom Stoppard, the author. Now 1977 is the year of Stephen Jeffreys.
>
> His masterpiece is a play lasting only 50 minutes. Having seen it, I went to see it again. Now I have read it.
>
> *Like Dolls or Angels* is not just funny and fierce and ablaze with surprises, it is wildly original and extraordinarily touching. I cannot get its two characters out of my head.
>
> Good drama observes characters at either end of their tether, be it Macbeth or Lord Babs. It shows what happens round the corner we dread to turn. Here we see what happens to Zuki, the cool Roedean dropout with the marvellous body—athlete, dare-devil and cynic. She gets a job riding bikes in a failing stunt show run by Hannigan, a girl-chasing brute with a crazy idea.
>
> As a publicity stunt he builds a giant catapult, sweating blood over optimum curves and ballistics, and shoots Zuki 200 feet across the Severn . . .
>
> The play rises higher still to become a metaphor for the daily, perennial struggle within us between ideas that go whoosh up in the air and apprehensions that go kersplatt on the pavement. If I cannot get Jeffreys's couple out of my mind, it is because I was born with both of them inside me. It took his genius to give them vivid identity.

The 1977 Edinburgh Fringe will be remembered for much else. *Private Dick* by Roger Michell and Richard Maher, a brilliant short piece about Raymond Chandler, Philip Marlowe and Humphrey Bogart. *Future Shock* a 'living magazine' based on the book by Alvin Toffler—an exercise in rock theatre, rather than a rock musical with a plot which included songs superimposed on it. *Ludwig and Bertie* by two Edinburgh writers Steve Cook and Justin Greene, revolved around Bertie Wooster, Bertram Russell, Ludwig Wittgenstein and Jeeves. The 1977 Fringe will be remembered by more people than the

1967 Fringe or the 1957 Fringe. It will also be noticed as the origin, as Robert Kemp said right at the beginning of this book, of much that is fresh in drama.

It would be unhelpful at this point to attempt anything resembling a summary or conclusion. The key to the Fringe is the philosophy of the Fringe Society:

> Artists come to this city to do their own thing at their own risk, with the maximum of help and the minimum of interference from this Society. Any form of quality control is either by the artists themselves or their public, in a direct, immediate one-to-one relationship, with no middlemen. The essential quality of the Fringe is its spontaneity and complete artistic freedom, and any attempt to contain it within formal limits, either of size or quality, would be to kill its essential spirit.
>
> Judging by its phenomenal growth since 1970, it would seem that this direct relationship between artists and their public is a healthy, honest, happy one. Long may both parties continue to enjoy each other. Congratulations to the artists on your Programme and congratulations to Edinburgh and its visitors on your Fringe.

from the Introduction to the
1976 Fringe Programme, Alistair Moffat

With its established administration smoothing the way to the groups' and the public's enjoyment as each year goes by, the Fringe Society maintains its attitude that it will never turn anyone away; it will always encourage new ideas however unlikely they may sound. The Fringe Society will continue to be responsible for bringing the public and the groups together, and that is all. This book is only a record of the first instalments of a story which, hopefully, has no end.

Cartoon by Michael Heath. 'He's been trying to see all the Fringe shows.'

Reproduced courtesy of Punch

Richard Crane on the Fringe

Edinburgh is a very personal and emotive place for me. More has happened for me in Edinburgh than anywhere else. The air is stimulating and refreshing, and always encourages me to take gigantic risks. In Edinburgh, I have always dared do things I would have thought twice about—even in Bradford—perhaps because the Festival, and with it the Fringe, explodes as the climax to a year's work, when there is less to lose and everything to gain. Also, it is only three short weeks of intense industry and competition. You have to make a fast and ferocious impact, and give all you have got, and more, into ensuring that your enthusiasm is immediately infectious. The Fringe is a loud and blinding firework. You light a fuse, and stand close.

I came to the Fringe by accident in 1971. I had avoided it at Cambridge in the mid-Sixties, when the general view was that Edinburgh was too crowded and a bit common for the serious theatre aspirant—a fixture for the Footlights 'B' team, while we, the cream, played politely and sank without trace, at Averham and Bury St Edmunds. Bradford University discovered the fallacy of this view, and romped to success in 1970 and 1971 with a barrage of new work ignited by Chris Parr at the Crown, next to the old Fringe Centre. More significant, the Bradford success of 1970 had generated the Pool, Edinburgh's year-round professional lunchtime theatre. I went there to do a play in June 1971 for a fortnight and no money. Four months later, I had been premiered three times on the Fringe, acted with Lindsay Kemp, featured in the terminal episodes of STV's *High Living*, and made two films—with a bull at Cape Wrath, and with Bette Davis on the Isle of Mull. Edinburgh takes you by surprise and makes you work. It was a bump coming back to England.

The next year, I wrote and acted again at the Pool. Plans for Bradford to transform the Wireworks, off the High Street, into a venue for unprecedented extravaganza were scotched (or 'englished') when the University finances decreed there was no 'brass in our muck', and my play about the Brontës had to wait a year before being shown under the NSDF umbrella at the YWCA in 1973. That year, we played the full festival with four premieres and one revival, declined a royal summons to amuse Princess Margaret, and ate and slept, as usual, like sweating sardines in a two-room flat.

1974 was my last Fringe as Fellow in Theatre at Bradford. I decided to stake my everything on the biggest spectacle I could think of. We had three days to transform Lauriston Hall into a jousting track and battlefield for Arthur and the knights and ladies of *The Quest*. In a company of sixty, we had as many engineers as actors. It was a demonstration of theatre as a composite art, with contributions coming from music, literature, heraldry, athletics, catering and scaffolding erection. It was a costly venture by Fringe standards. Bradford University provides an annual grant for its drama group, which has to be carefully husbanded. Two forces are at work in the group's financial policy: *1* to break even whenever possible, with low-budget lunchtime and late-night shows supporting the large scale productions, and *2* to keep seat prices minimal. The risk with *The Quest* was that two-thirds of the annual budget was expended before the show opened, and could only be recouped if we did 120 percent business. This kind of necessity is the mother of the Fringe—a belief in miracles offset by a tendency, in the heat of preparation, to overlook basic formalities. In this instance, we had failed to spot the difference between an entertainment and a theatre license, and through my chain mail on the first night, I spied two grim figures by the door with tight lips and tensing knuckles. The police had come to close the show after only one performance. The next day, we went to the City Chambers, and didn't leave until we were legal. It was touch and go, and many steely Scottish precepts had to be bent. The episode has served as a cautionary tale to all Fringe companies who make light of licenses.

Edinburgh means as much to me personally as professionally. I was succeeded at Bradford by Faynia Williams. She joined the Fringe Board of Directors. We met at Board meetings—always lively and productive punctuations in a busy year's paragraph—decided to collaborate on a show for Bradford at the Fringe, and married at South Queensferry under the Forth Bridge, while *Clownmaker* was playing at Lauriston Hall.

The next year, Bradford went to Poland instead of Edinburgh. I did a play for the Traverse, and Faynia did one for Richard Demarco. In 1977, Bradford came back with *Satan's Ball*. We sat in the Old Chaplaincy for an afternoon, before a word of the play was written. The building is dominated by majestic organ pipes; the height of the roof is about thirty feet. The play was designed there and then, on floating discs spiralling up to the full height, the whole supported on a forest of scaffolding which raised the floor of the hall to the level of the balcony. I can't think of anywhere else where this kind of adventure can be followed through so suddenly and so easily, on such limited resources. At a time when theatres elsewhere were commissioning two- or three-handers with one set and no music, we had a free hand to mount a show with all the hazards and spectacle of a circus.

It is wrong, though, to dwell on old Fringes. The day Fringe audiences develop memories, or even expectations, the Fringe will have become established, and a Fringe of the Fringe will become necessary to keep the thing young. This is the constant danger—that the Fringe, now quite an elderly parasite, on which the main Festival to a large extent depends, will become secure. It has to continue rough-hewn and spontaneous with a constant influx of new talent. It is unique in the world for being deliberately unorganised. No-one is invited by the Fringe Society to perform. No-one is sponsored. Services are supplied with the impartiality of a telephone directory. The Fringe should have no past and no future, but a bounding present that goes on and on.

Richard Crane, 1978

Richard Crane wrote *Clownmaker, The Quest, Satan's Ball* and he has been Fellow in Theatre at Bradford University and Writer in Residence at the National Theatre.

 **Leslie Bennie**

From a professional standpoint as opposed to that of the disinterested spectator, the dominating remaining memory of the Traverse is undoubtedly finance—or more accurately the distinct lack of it. The time immemorial clash between art and business has never before been so dramatically staged as it was between the artistic group who based its policy on the ideal, and the financial group who tried in vain to pin that policy to some kind of reality. Compromises were rarely if ever attempted: the impossible always won through. The question still being asked by those who came through those days of trauma, intrigue and failure is how did the Traverse—and indeed the Demarco gallery—survive:

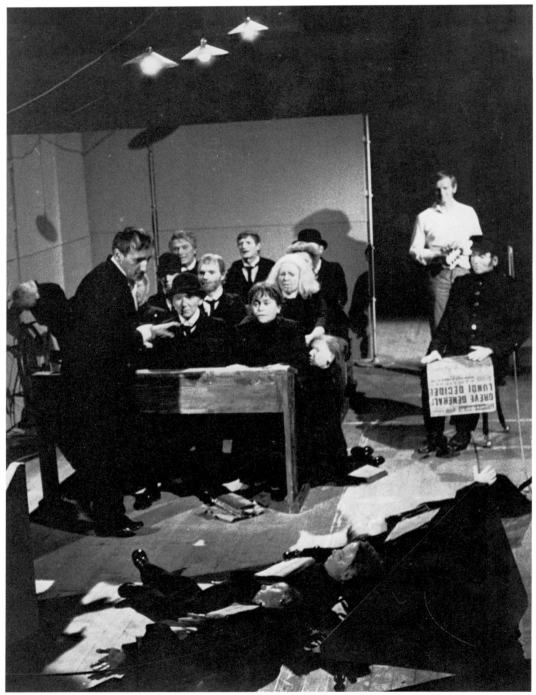

A scene from *The Dead Class* **performed by Cricot Theatre II from Poland at the 1976 Fringe. Tadeusz Kantor, the director, was on stage throughout the play. He is standing on the left of the picture**

in retrospect the answer may lie in the patrons' conviction that nothing and nobody could ever destroy their respective vehicles. Such a bland explanation would unfortunately conceal the enormous if not unparalleled contribution made by private and public subscription in the form of not only money but also of service chattels and advice, not forgetting the unbelievably generous and untiring giving of time—often to the extent of abdicating the personal, indeed the business life.

In 1978 it is difficult to conceive the Traverse Theatre Club as anything other than solid, environmentally and financially. Its attributes are so at variance with the recent past; landlord instead of insecure tenant, benefactor rather than impecunious recipient, mentor not immature mentee. In the late 1960s after a series of uniquely created financial disasters, notably the Barrie Halls episode, the Traverse Theatre Club faced extinction through plain insolvency. The choice of the word unique is deliberate—it is at the very least highly unusual to run a privately sponsored lottery at a loss, to sell paintings at a loss and perhaps the most spectacular, to produce losses from a fruit machine (in 1968).

Ignored in the main by the press, except to condemn it, despised by councillors (some of whom had heard of it but none, it is alleged, had ever crossed the threshold), and suffering from a falling membership, the Traverse presented a poor, almost negative, case.

A special meeting was called in early 1969, the substance of which was generally thought to be closure; the agenda, however, was 'new premises'. Hence the move from Lawnmarket to Grassmarket. There with greater commitments, including a more onerous rent imposed and exacted by a less lenient landlord, the Traverse fared little better financially. The same theme continued—a continual yet losing battle to meet not only suppliers' bills but also weekly payments, highlighted on Fridays by frantically running around the Lothians looking for someone, anyone to cover the wages cheque until the following Tuesday. Also to be continued were the endless meetings with bankers, Art Council, and debt collectors. Other inheritances from the Lawnmarket were the alternate opening and closing of the restaurant, and the by now legendary losses in the bar—the major turnover of which was staff.

An outsider attending a Traverse committee meeting would put as last on a list of objective choices, that what he had witnessed represented a theatre. Gradually, however, through its artistic direction, things began to change. Reputations were established; the subsidised loss-making objective turned into the notion of 'break-even' and very quickly this possibility was followed by a surplus-making objective. (This move was hastened by the Scottish Arts Council policy of deficit grant funding, which is a device purporting to match internally generated surpluses with a similar amount, thus overnight doubling the surplus.) Thus continues the Traverse.

Much the same may be said about the Demarco Gallery, except that with the Traverse Theatre Club the committee was usually aware that the decision would result in a financial loss; with the gallery losses always came as a surprise to the authors of the proposal or forecast. Although, after many years and many losses, some of the excitement was taken out of the surprise.

Leslie Bennie, 1978

Leslie Bennie lectures in accountancy at the Heriot Watt University in Edinburgh. He has been a financial adviser/accountant/treasurer to the early Traverse Theatre Club, the Richard Demarco Gallery, John Calder's Ledlanet Nights near Milnathort in Fife, and is currently the Treasurer of the Festival Fringe Society.

Appendix A
'The Scotsman' Fringe Firsts
1973 to 1977

1973
Onstage 66—*Man of Sorrows* by Toppano, Mortimer and Desmond
Traverse Theatre Club—*Union Jack and Bonzo* by Stanley Eveling
Pool Lunch Hour Theatre Club—omnibus award for so many new productions
Bradford University Drama Group—*Thunder* by Richard Crane
Scottish Theatre Ballet—*Japanese Dances* by Jack Carter
Pilobolus Dance Theater—group devised works
Stephanie Rich—*Sarah Bernhardt* by Stephanie Rich
Cricot Theatre—*Lovelies and Dowdies* by Tadeusz Kantor
Western Canada Theatre Company—*The Ecstasy of Rita Joe* by George Ryga

1974
Bradford University Drama Group—*The Quest* by Richard Crane
Russell Hunter—*Knox* by W. Gordon Smith
Zforzando—*Shylock* by Roger Haynes and Paul Bentley
Tangent Theatre Company—*The Creation of the World and Other Business* by Arthur
   Miller
Pool Lunch Hour Theatre Club—*Stallerhof* by Kreutz
Mitchell's Theatre Gymnasium—*The Archangel Michael* by Georgi Markov
Opera Sigma—Hugh Miller by Colin macLean and Reginald Barrett-Ayres
Strathclyde Theatre Group—*The Golden City* by Hugo Gifford and the company
Traverse Theatre Club—*Schippel* by C. P. Taylor
Freies Theater Munchen—*After Brecht* devised by George Froscher and the company
Matt Mattox Jazzart Dance Company—*Jazzart* by Matt Mattox
Pool Lunch Hour Theatre Club—*Drumbuie/Faustus* by John Abulafia and *Edgar Allan's
   Late Night Horror* by Robert Nye

1975
Bradford Theatre Group— *Clownmaker* by Richard Crane
Traverse Theatre Club—*Moon* devised and performed by Annie Stainer
Moubray Productions—*Morecambe* by Kreutz
Yves Marc and Claire Heggen—*The Mutants* devised and performed by them

1976
Mime Amiel—*Un Jour La Terre* devised and performed by Jean-Pierre Amiel
Aberdeen Studio Theatre Group—*An Exotic in Edinburgh* by John Irvine
GeVa Company—*The Contrast* by Royall Tyler
Leonard Maguire—*The Wasting of Dunbar* by Leonard Maguire

The Entertainment Machine—*The Farndale Avenue Housing Estate Townswomens' Guild Dramatic Society's Production of Macbeth* by David McGillivray and Walter Zerlin
Paines Plough—*Music to Murder By* by David Pownall
West Midlands Umbrella Group—*Woody Shavings* and *Sir Herbert MacRae* by the company
Joint Stock—*Light Shining in Buckinghamshire* by Caryl Churchill
Playback Theatre—*Tapestries A Travesty* by the company
Malenkaia Theatre Company—*Mockhero's Heron* by Stuart Delves
Cricot Theatre II—*The Dead Class* by Tadeusz Kantor
Chris Langham's Frenzshow—*Tea With Dick and Jerry* by Bill Schoppert
Shared Experience—*The Third Arabian Night* devised by the company
Belmont School—*The Ballad of Salomon Pavey* by Jeremy James Taylor and David Drew-Smythe

1977
John Bett, Alex Norton and Bill Paterson—*Writer's Cramp* by John Byrne
Leonard Maguire—*Navigator in the Seventh Circle* by Leonard Maguire
Annie Stainer and Emil Wolk—*The Ancient Mariner* devised by the company
Paines Plough—*Richard III Part Two* by David Pownall
Harry Stamper—*Recollections Between The Wars* by Harry Stamper
Anglo-French Productions—*Player King* by Patrick Williams
Bradford University Drama Group—*Satan's Ball* by Richard Crane
Borderline Theatre—*When Hair Was Long And Time Was Short* by Billy Connolly
Hull Truck—*Bed of Roses* by Mike Bradwell
Bristol Revunions—*A Respectable Family* by Maxim Gorky
Traverse Theatre Club—*Walter* by C. P. Taylor
Pirate Jenny—*Whistling At Milestones* by Alex Glasgow
Cambridge Mummers—*Private Dick* by Richard Maher

 # Appendix B

Temporary Theatre. Bradford University Drama Group at the Old Chaplaincy Centre, Forrest Road.

Nobody goes to a Fringe show if they do not think they will enjoy what they see, no-one goes to be seen there, or because it is the 'done thing'. Of all types of theatre, the Fringe concentrates most exclusively on what happens on stage or in the playing area.

The reason for that is that most Fringe shows are done in places primarily designed for something else. In this set of illustrations you can see how Bradford University transformed the Old Chaplaincy Centre into a theatre. The designer of the set is Faynia Williams, one of many experts in constructing temporary theatres using techniques which can be seen at their best at the Edinburgh Fringe. The conversion of the Old Chaplaincy Centre is a spectacular example of these skills in action.

**The conversion of the Old Chaplaincy
Centre by Bradford**

 # Index

123

Illustrations are referred to by italicized figures